THE DEATH PROJECT

An Anthology for These Times

Edited by Gretchen Eick and Cora Poage

Blue Cedar Press

Copyright © Blue Cedar Press, 2020
All rights reserved. No part of this book may be reproduced in any form without written permission from the publisher:
Blue Cedar Press
PO Box 48715
Wichita, KS 67201.

ISBN: 978-1-7342272-6-0---paperback (Ingram and Amazon kdp)
ISBN: 978-1-7342272-7-7 ebook (Ingram epub)

Cover photo: Michael Poage
Composition: MD. Hasanur Rahman
Editors: Gretchen Eick and Cora Poage
Items previously published are used by permission and previous publication noted.

Printed in the United States of America

Table of Contents

Introduction by Gretchen Eick 6

Families and Loss 9
   A Mother's Kiss by Amena Mohamad 10
   Sonnet for Stephanie by Janet Jenkins-Stotts 13
   What are we waiting for? By Cora Poage 14
   Requiem for My Brother by Edward Ernest Goode 17
   From the Beginning and the Eve by Maaskelah Kimit Thomas . .20
   Early December by Julie Ann Baker Brin 23
   Father's Day by Diane Wahto 24
   Tone Deaf by Julie Ann Baker Brin .26
   Stroke Midnight by Julie Ann Baker Brin 27
   The Brother by Ruth Maus 28

Black Lives Matter 29
   Black Lives Matter by Donald Betts, Jr. 30
   My Name is George Floyd Today! by Eyyup Essen 33
   June 2020 by David Stewart 34
   Family Tries to Cope...by Mark E. McCormick 36

War and Violence 38
   Going Down by Aida Dziho-Sator .39
   Yes the Killers by Robert L. Dean, Jr. 41
   Newtown, Connecticut by Judy Keller Hatteberg 43
   The Quandary Najiyah Maxfield 44
   Soldier's Christmas by Mark Scheel .50
   Carnage by Najiyah Maxfield 52
   Coming Home from Iraq by Mark Scheel 57

Suicide 58
   Mother's Suicide by Ronda Miller 59
   A Child's First Rose by George Hough 63
   A Permanent Solution to a Temporary Problem by Jim Potter . . .70

COVID-19 a novel corona virus 74
    Virus by Michael D. Graves 75
    Fist in the Air by Michael Poage. 77
    Night Quarantine by Gretchen Eick 78

The Process of Dying 80
    The Trip by Linda Gebert 81
    The Only Peace Is a Painful One by Mark McCormick 83
    Hank's Last Night by Susan Moir 86
    Departing by Gretchen Eick 87
    Spacemen by Robert L. Dean, Jr. 97
    A Good Life by Judy Keller Hatteberg 100
    Mother's Fears by Janet Jenkins-Stotts. 101
    As I Grow Older by Michael Poage 102
    Death Happens by Bill Dee Johnston .103

Grief and Remembrance 104
    Endlessness by Julie Ann Baker Brin .105
    Grief by Jeani Rice-Cranford 108
    Ali: Speaking to... by Many by Mark E. McCormick 111
    Clean up on Aisle Five by Robert L. Dean, Jr. 114
    No Words by Cammie Funston 116
    Grief and Music by Cora Poage 118
    Sanders Blindsided...by Mark E. McCormick 122
    Suite for the Bull and the Fairy by Susan Moir 125
    To Remember by Richard Eick. 127

Death Professionals. 128
    Living Death by Jim Potter 129
    Bedside Cathedral by John Monroe-Cassel 135
    The Death Trade by Gretchen Eick. 137
    Interview with a Mortician: by Jim Potter 144

Rituals and Religion 151
    A Ritual Libations for...by Maaskelah Kimit Thomas 152
    Assisi Pilgrimage by Julie Stielstra. 155

I Sleep with the Dead by Mark Scheel 159
Death in the Jewish Tradition 161
The Viewing by Robert L. Dean, Jr. 165
How to Bury a Saint by Miriam Iwashige 167
Concept of Death among Hindus by Mohan Kambampati... 170
A Silent Gathering by Judy Keller Hatteberg 172
From *The Soul of the Indian* by Charles Ohiyesa Eastman .. 173
between living and dying by Erin Kyna 174
The Grief Gap by German Theologian Dietrich Bonhoeffer . 176
Death in Islam....................................... 177
A Roadmap to Comfort...by Sharon Hill Cranford........ 179
Words of Greeting at...by Richard Eick 181
Baha'i Teachings on Death by Philip Wood 183
Please, can we be Mexican? by Gretchen Eick........... 187

Letting Go 189
My Sweet, Crushed Angel by Hafiz 190
'Where Everything Is Music' by Rumi................. 191
Sorrow Kite by Cammie Funston 193

Epilogue by Cora Poage........................... 194

About the Authors............................... 197

Introduction

This book began in early April 2020. It seemed the world was short on emotional resources to cope with the scale of death this pandemic of COVID-19, the novel corona virus, was producing. In U.S. culture, people view death multiple times a week in crime dramas and participate in "taking out" others in video games. Yet most people have not seen a dead body, other than their deceased pets, until aged parents die. The popular culture tells them to "get over it" quickly when they lose a family member.

"Denial is not an effective life strategy," Andrew Cuomo, the governor of New York, told the world as his state struggled to cope with unprecedented numbers of deaths, inadequate protective gear for hospital workers, and overwhelmed mortuaries.

Denial was totally ineffective as the numbers rose, and later, when some communities opened bars and churches and (some) people eagerly embraced their former social lives…and the numbers of the infected grew and one thousand Americans a day died of the virus. But denial was our cultural default, that and secret terror.

I talked with life coach and spiritual counselor Cora Poage, who happens to be my daughter, about what we might do to help people cope in this time. What if we gathered the experiences of ordinary people whose lives had been profoundly altered by deaths, people who had found ways to reorder their lives and find meaning, or at least some sort of solace, in this experience that none of us can avoid.

The board of Blue Cedar Press, a small independent press based in Wichita, Kansas, agreed to my proposal to invite anyone interested to submit pieces they had written about this much-avoided subject for possible inclusion in an anthology. The deadline was July with hopes to have a book in print by late August. Neither contributors nor the press would profit from this "happening." Proceeds above the cost of publication would go to health care workers combating the phenomenon transforming the world of 2020-21.

The number and diversity of submissions moved us. They came from Australia, Turkey, and Bosnia and Herzegovina; from Muslims, Christians, Hindus, Baha'is, modern mystics, and agnostics; published writers and new voices.

You will find here stories, poems, memories, and essays that address the many aspects of death, including losing family members to different ways of dying; the process of grieving and letting go; the disproportionate number of Black people dying at the hands of police; the ravages of COVID-19 across the globe; and the despair that grows suicide.

We hope that you will be nourished as you look through others' eyes at what none of us can avoid. We hope your empathy will expand as you learn how different religious groups address death and how people -- including "death professionals" -- cope. Among the gems submitted was a poem to share with children who are grieving.

May this book help you find solace and encouragement as you navigate the deep feelings and anxieties stirred inside us by this extraordinary time, and may you discover the strength that comes from feeling, sharing, and helping others heal.

Gretchen Eick

A Mother's Kiss

He lay motionless on his parents' bed. It was like he was taking a nap. I thought I could see his small chest rising and falling as if he was breathing. For a moment, I thought they had made a mistake. At least, I hoped that they had.

The mother, her sisters, friends, and neighbors from around the village gathered in the master's bedroom. There, in his parents' room, we stood over the little boy and cried silently. Even though it was expected, everyone was startled by what they witnessed. The child's nanny looked at him like a mother would at the sight of a loved one; she cried for the little boy she once looked after and eventually loved.

In the summer of 2016, I took a trip to my husband's country of Lebanon. We stayed in a village called Houmine Tahta about an hour south of the Capital, Beirut. We were there but a week when we received word that his cousin's child had died. He had cancer. Standing there in a stranger's bedroom, I couldn't help but to be mesmerized by what I saw. He just lay there on a king size bed in a room partially lined with curtains. They hung from the top of the high window and flowed downward barely touching the patterned tiled floors. The curtains protected us from the summer's heat, making the room dark and cool. However, they did not protect us from the truth of what had unfolded in front of us.

Families and Loss

We were then directed to leave the room. The mother wanted to lie next to her son for the last time. The men were in the living room drinking Turkish coffee and smoking cigarettes. A week prior, they were all together in the same room mourning the loss of the boy's grandfather.

The women went into a separate living space to have Turkish coffee and smoke too. I found myself in a large and wide hallway unsure of where I wanted to go. I then proceeded outside thinking that maybe I could go home. Above me, vines of grapes stewed in the sun's heat turning their fruit from undesirably sour to irresistibly sweet. Up ahead I could see people talking amongst themselves waiting around, unsure of what to do, uncomfortable. We all looked up in the same direction when we heard tires and gravel meet. There it came. The small village ambulance that would take the little boy to his final bed. We were immersed in thick grey clouds, even though the sun was stunningly hot and bright.

As if the reality of the situation wasn't surreal enough, the father, hesitantly stepped out of his home holding his son's wrapped lifeless body and moved towards the ambulance. He stepped up into the ambulance holding his son tightly against his chest, sat down and glared out the double doors. The rest of us just stood silent.

Just as the ambulance pulled out to leave, the little boy's mother ran out of the house, unable to handle the momentary separation from her son. For a moment, I envisioned the many times she had jumped when she heard his cries after he had scraped his knee on gravel or when he had bumped his head on the table while chasing his siblings around the house. Now for the last time, as if she heard him cry, she ran out of her home wrapped in a traditional long and flowing black dress that followed her towards the slow-moving ambulance. She quickly stepped into the ambulance and scooped her son out of her husband's arms into her own. I imagined that she realized in that very moment that she would no longer be able to console him, cradle him, and kiss his boo-boos. For the last time, before she placed him down into the earth next to his grandfather in the century-old Houmine Tahta Cemetery, she leaned over and gently kissed him.

By Amena Mohamad

SONNET FOR STEPHANIE

It's not right. The last born should not die first.

Love for our little sister couldn't surrender

Her tenuous life for what we feared the worst.

Our hopes for recovery, although slender,

Asked her to endure radiation and pain

For us. Our fear of loss tried to smother

Her certain choice as we watched her life wane.

"Don't go," we all pleaded, but she had other,

Braver plans, to gather the reins of death

Into her own frail hands and jump the last,

The highest, hurdle on her ending breath,

Knowing she would land, where in years past

Her loved ones had landed, in a sacred place,

A landing blind, but sure, guided by grace.

by Janet Jenkins-Stotts

What are we waiting for?

My grandfather softened as Alzheimer's began to take over his Being. As if his heart and his mouth became One.

"You know you've always been my favorite." He said to me once with a glint in his eye.

I smiled, feeling like maybe he said this to all of the grandkids, and actually part of me hoping everyone was being bathed in this much grandfatherly light. Don't we all deserve that? At least one moment where the Giant of a Man in our lives gives us the approval we have sought for one way or the other from birth.

Almost like God saying, "You are good enough."

I felt my body relax as if I could finally breathe. Maybe even for the first time.

My grandfather lived Love in those final days, and liked to give me unsolicited advice.

"You know Cora." He said, "You are only ready to be in a romantic partnership when you know you'd be great on your own."

He looked at my Grandmother Liz, his wife of 56 years, and said. "Liz you would have been great on your own."

With tears in her eyes, she said, "Only half as great."

but I was able to share the story of how Love lasts, of my Grandfather being here in spirit for my sister's ceremony, of my grandparents always connected. I just had to hold on to the table in front of me so I didn't fall over.

A few days before my grandfather passed away, he looked at my grandmother and said, "I don't know who you are, but I sure do Love you."

Sometimes it takes an excessive amount of champagne to help us be vulnerable, to share love, other times it takes an Alzheimer's diagnosis. But whatever it is, let it move you. Let it wake you up.

Allow your heart and mouth to become one.

Tell them you love them.

I mean really, What are we waiting for?

by Cora Poage

I was 19, such a kid, and yet I could still see what happened to our family when we let our hearts be heard. When we stopped trying to be cool and collected and independent and suave and just LIVED LOVE.

My grandparents melted into each other that day. I saw it. Love loving Love.

I was studying abroad in Australia, asleep in my dorm room, when the wind blowing through the curtains shocked me straight up in my bed. I looked around.

"He's gone" I think I said the words out loud.

And the next day, I found out it was true.

My sister got married that fall. I shared a room with my grandmother. She was in deep mourning. The morning of the wedding I woke up to the sounds of a palm tree being delivered to the hotel courtyard by helicopter. I looked over and could see my grandmother and another man sitting in the arm chairs overlooking the window, watching the delivery.

Later that day I said, Tutu, I saw you and Uncle John watching the palm tree this morning.

She looked at me perplexed, "Uncle John? He wasn't there. It was just me."

Shivers overtook my body. Granddad was here. With her. With us. At my sister's wedding. Helping all of us open our hearts to love more and more.

I drank too much before the wedding and sobbed embarrassingly through the entire ceremony and then made a frighteningly obnoxious Maid of Honor Toast,

Requiem for My Brother

When my telephone rang at 5am or so Tuesday, December 3, I was surprised to hear the caller tell me that Lewis Goode was unresponsive. She was calling from the Bay Area nursing home that his daughter found for him a couple of years earlier.

"Unresponsive"? I couldn't imagine my brother being unresponsive; he was always "the life of the party", the teen whose saxophone playing made his ambition to be "an entertainer" seem a reasonable ambition. Of the two of us, he was the one who mastered the Erector Set challenge, painted by numbers, adopted goldfish, and persuaded our parents to get us puppies, a brown one for him and a black one for me. Lewis was my only brother; 15 months separated our birthdays, but though we were enough alike as boys to hear adults ask if we were twins--he fat and me skinny--we were as different in character as our pets were in color.

Some might say our relationship was marred by sibling rivalry, I'd say, my jealousy. I envied him the spotlight he owned, the dance steps he commanded, and the friends he kept in his orbit. I had none of those qualities.

Though we slept in the same room, we went our separate ways when awake. I'd be the first to leave for school, so I'd get home early enough to see him dressed in a shirt, jacket or tie that was mine. So I'd attack saying, *"Don't wear my stuff!"* We'd run through the apartment with Lewis tossing anything including chairs to prevent me from pummeling him hard and fast as punishment for wearing or using my stuff. Though he always lost those fights, he'd continue to wear or use something of mine whenever he wanted to.

Our family knew our fraternal connection wasn't ideal. I remember our mother telling us not to fight and as we got older to remember to give each other birthday gifts. Thank God or Madeline Goode or both that we were faithful to each other on that score.

We both moved away from Boston after graduating high school. Lewis entered the Air Force and afterwards came back as damaged goods. Alcohol was a crutch and unpaid loans as well as larceny a source of cash. I don't remember when we actually stopped fighting. We never connected as I imagine other siblings connect, but we always remembered each other's birthday. He had a knack for selecting just the card whose humorous message communicated a truth so profound that absorbing it would cause my heart to skip a beat and my breathing to deepen.

Our parents divorced before I began first grade and though we boys were required visit our father and our paternal grandparents on Sundays, Daddy never paid any real attention to us except for the time he gave us a significant portion of his model railroad setup. Francis Goode wasn't a good Dad.

It turns out Lewis was a model Dad. His daughter, Rima, was so much a "Daddy's girl" that after she found him living in Kansas City in squalor that broke her heart, she found a Bay Area nursing home near enough to where she lived in Berkley to enable twice a week visits. There were

From the Beginning and the Eve

From an early age, I have been fascinated with the Madonna concept. I can remember doodling images in the margins of school work, feeble attempts at sketches and sculpting in playdough and clay. But never the serene white queen watching placidly over her equally pale charge. In my deepest self, I always envisioned the original Madonna as black, that first woman, who didn't have the benefit of a mother to instruct her in the ways of womanhood and motherhood. She was simply created and expected to know and understand her role. And she obviously did. Like first nature, she knew enough to grow into herself. She loved from her depths the sons and daughters who emerged from her womb; watched with wonder as each one was quickened with life and spirit, and instinctively created space within her world for them to grow, each one in her/his own time and way, and ultimately into her or his ownself.

Instinctively, she gave the sons to their father, but not before she'd imparted some of what was strong in her, and some of what was gentle, both elements of the same essence, both tempered with wisdom and love. Her hope was that they would cherish and shelter that which she had carefully imparted. Her dream was that it would flow with their seed to future sons and future worlds. She was, after all, a mother --- the beginning and the eve.

And to her daughters, dark and delicate, she sang. Love songs and struggle songs. Morning songs and blood songs.

days when he was so desperate for his drinking buddies that he accused Rima of kidnapping him, but Rima wasn't intimidated; she wanted the best for her father and provided him with accommodation in the nursing home, along with treats for his sweet tooth, and day trips to spice up his life.

There was no funeral; his body was cremated and then buried. I've kept many of his birthday cards and will sigh a special sigh when I get no birthday card from my brother this month and again on September 13 when I will send no birthday card to Lewis.

By Edward Ernest Goode

realize that I could choose the woman I would be. And so, from that day forth, I daily made the choice. Woman I am. My songs are my own, rhythms and tones uniquely mine: some weak, some strong, but growing clearer and more melodic with each passing day.

Every once in a while, though, I catch myself singing the melody of a song I've heard another woman sing, my ear resting peacefully beneath her heart, my heart attuned so perfectly with her peace. A mother's song. Near and deep. From the beginning and the eve.

By Maaskelah Kimit Thomas

Analytical and precise. Always and with purpose. For they were the daughters of the morning, and the mothers of future dawns. And where she'd had no instruction herself, she knew they too could survive without it. But instinct made her sing her songs, no matter, even while knowing that the music in her being was also partly theirs. She watched her daughters grow, and she grew, too, new and still becoming. And when the first daughter gave birth to life, she felt her own delivery pains anew and intensified. And knew herself --- woman/mother --- the beginning and the eve.

My own mother died when I was very young. I never quite understood or believed that she was actually gone for good. I used to pray at day's end that she might come to me in my restless dreams, but she never did. I can even remember moments of shame because she wasn't there. (I once lied to a schoolmate and told him that she'd been eaten by a lion. After all, only the most heinous of circumstances could account for a mother not being there for her children; death by illness never seemed quite heinous or justifiable enough.)

I didn't really miss her though, until I reached my teens. I turned one day, to ask a question that only a mother can answer for her daughter. I don't remember what the question was --- maybe about boys or men or love; maybe about baking bread --- but I do remember my pain and sorrow and anger that she just was not there. And wouldn't ever be again. It was then that I realized that it was up to me to mother me. And I began, at that moment, to draw on the spirit of the First Mother who, like me, was motherless and on her own. I found that ever-growing space inside myself and sat awhile to ponder what being woman meant. I looked around me at other women and felt a measure of relief to

EARLY DECEMBER

How on earth we did
the things we needed
to do I'll never know. Mom sewed
the missing sequins on
my funeral blouse. I went
through the photo drawers;
Brother picked through
Dad's clothes
and we all had lunch
with the grave digger.

Looking back it seems so cold
to have completed
our expected tasks.
Better that we should have all
fallen to the ground
in mourning and never have
gotten the deed done.

By Julie Ann Baker Brin
Published in *Sheridan Edwards Review*, Vol. 19
(Newman University, 2011)

Father's Day

On my front porch,
newly painted, newly red,
I drink coffee as I did
in summers past,
at my father's house
on the porch
he built and painted red.
Mom and I would talk
of woman things,
cooking, cleaning,
hormones, depression,
men, while Dad mowed the lawn,
cleaned out the shed.

Chores finished,
he sat with us,
smoking his cigar.

The disease came fast
with no reprieve.
I, too far away to lend a hand,
our mother too far gone
to know how bad he was.
She knew only that he must
walk down the hall,
the one he built when
he added rooms to the house.

The last he heard
of me was a shout,
a slammed door.

Not to make more
of it than it is,
he was not a temperate
man. He did the best
he could, given everything.
He taught me the mysteries
of my '47 Chevy engine,
how to use the choke
when it died
on cold mornings.

By Diane Wahto

TONE DEAF

I hope my Dad still

sings off-key

in Heaven, maintains

his imperfect perfection;

the things we used

to laugh about, now

Gabriel can, too.

By Julie Ann Baker Brin

STROKE MIDNIGHT

You could take an auger to your head
and it would barely leave a scar.
One farm accident after another.
Dozens of years of near-misses
and there you were. Just always
powerful, ox-strong, alive.

Then some little, tiny, clotted thing
stopped the blood into your brain
and made all of us powerless.

Not the David vs. Goliath story we wanted
to hear. All the method in the universe
won't help me figure this one out,
nor the logic of the antidote: pray
to the god who allowed it to happen.

By Julie Ann Baker Brin
Published in *Sheridan Edwards Review,* Vol. 18,
(Newman University 2010).

The Brother

A massive brain hemorrhage, said the coroner.
Two days undiscovered in his bed.
We broke into the house, how inconvenient.
The frumpy pillow shivering in red.

A nightstand radio aimlessly playing.
I blotted out the words until the song,
Something, something crushing with a hammer,
Asking *where had all the flowers gone?*

By Ruth Maus
Reprinted with permission from *Valentine*, published by Meadowlark Press.

Black Lives Matter

Black Lives Matter

My Brother and I came from the same value system, raised under the same roof but took two separate paths for similar reasons.

My parents married soon after high school graduation, our father joined the army, and they started a family.

Our life took us from a place of family violence and homelessness in Kansas, to the innercity ghettos of Las Vegas.

To understand our journey, you would have to know our struggle. Our family fell apart early, and the three of us fell into an oppressive system that did not offer many avenues of escape.

I had always felt that I needed to step-up where my father stepped out. So, I had to grow up quickly. I felt it my duty to protect my family in an environment of economic decline where gangs were rife, and gun shots were heard throughout the night (like a war zone).

What we witnessed as young boys became more traumatic as we grew older, and the systematic way of life became our everyday reality, which meant all three of us needed to learn how to survive collectively, and individually. My way of survival was to work full time in the Casinos at age 16 while attending school, and remaining actively involved so as to claw my way out, from a system designed to swallow me in.

The difference is that I was able to escape first, but barely, and with the help of teachers, mentors, and a diverse group of friends, and colleagues, I sought outside the boundaries of the complex.

While Ron (my younger brother) for whom I've always felt responsible was locked in an environment where signs of hope were only a glimmer appearing from behind the mountains. He felt like he needed to be there to protect us, but more so our mother within the confines of the complex. A feeling we have often shared with each other. Everyday there was news of someone we knew of that was either shot, murdered or taken to jail. Police were ever present, and that fear of being detained, arrested or pulled over was breathtaking, and an everyday reality. The fear has just only subsided in me, since moving to Australia.

My brother adopted the survival of the fittest tactics of a community that did not visually show signs of escape but one that meant picking a side, demonstrating loyalty, and gaining respect. As much as we were sheltered by our mother, she could not keep us locked in forever. We needed to figure out how to be men. At 16, I began working in the casinos after school, Ron succumbed to the peer pressure that led him to skip school and commit petty theft, eventually landing him in the" juvenile justice system. Ron's reputation within the complex provided some security to our family due to his affiliations, but was not enough to keep me from being robbed at gun point, or to prevent my mother's car window from being shot out, or my Uncle, a deacon in the church, from being murdered in the cross fires of a drive by shooting.

Ron escaped but not without experiencing early fatherhood, incarceration, and threats made on his life. He received his high school diploma while incarcerated. Just as he began to establish himself, he was brutally murdered in Kansas at age 33.

Until this day, I look back over my life and ask if there was something I could have done to get him to follow my path, but as I think back, he was only trying to survive the best way he knew how, under the circumstances of a system that has more black men in prison than there are in University.

I simply chose not to be another statistic, but that ambition alone wasn't enough to guarantee another day of life. It was only by grace and faith that I was not a systemic statistic.

When educational services, mentorship programs, job training, and employment are lacking, it opens the door to poverty, depression, violence, drugs, gangs, death, and racial profiling.

But in America it doesn't ease up just because you make it out. As I was quick to learn, even state Senators are racially profiled.

By former Kansas state senator Donald Betts, Jr.

June 2020

As people continue to gather, the church is a witness.
Windows boarded up
A silent sentinel but one that speaks loudly.
Witness to the desolating sacrilege just days before.

Pepper spray
Rubber bullets
Troopers on horseback
Prelude to the word made prop—
Not as a symbol of love
But of the will to "dominate."

Yet, people continue to gather
To cry out
To march
To kneel—8 minutes and 46 seconds—to kneel.

As the wall went up across the street, the church was a witness.
A wall of separation
A wall of fear
A wall of shame
The people cut off from the People's House
The wall—
Blank and barren—
Waiting for a word.

And the word came:
Black Lives Matter
I can't breathe

My Name is George Floyd Today!

My happiness cannot come out of selfishness
If my happiness is individual, it is hypocrisy
After George Floyd's killing, I cannot say my friends are safe!!
When George's family is crying, I cannot say "My family is doing great"
When someone is killed, all humanity should grieve
Oh mom, I think I can't breathe anymore
But, do not take my revenge by anger
Maybe my separation will bring liberation
Maybe it will be a wake-up call for humanity
Oh mom, I still do not hate anyone
You only taught me how to love people
They ask me to hate people
I can Breathe in hate
But I can only
Breathe out peace
You only taught me how to convert hate to love

To those who are ready to invade places
Say
You can only
Conquer hearts!
Have you heard of invaded hearts?!
Never
Ever
Peace does not come by coercion!

By Eyyup Essen

Say his name
Say her name
In paintings and posters, the word came
And covered the wall of shame.

The church is a witness as the people come
As the people march
As the people chant
As the people cry for justice
The church on H and 16th is a witness.
Are we?

By David Stewart

Family Tries to Cope after Inmate's Death

At a tidy little house on North Ash on Monday, cars lined the driveway and the street. Visitors walked in and out, some of them tearful. Some chatted with a tiny little girl who doesn't know what has happened.

Danielle Morris invited me in. She's 23 and remarkably calm a day after the death of her father, Alexis McCullough, an inmate at the work release center downtown. A witness and friend in the next bed said he died after hours of begging for help.

Danielle's newborn slept in one room, while the family scurried about in the next room, digging through a box of photographs for a photo fit for an obituary.

This is the scene people don't see. The other side. The scene of people grappling with a loss of someone like Danielle's dad, the best way they can. He'd landed in work release following arson and robbery convictions. Maybe, they wondered, he was the kind of man no one thought was important enough to listen to until it was too late.

Activity swirls around Danielle. Calls from me. Calls from television stations. Could we borrow a photo? Suddenly, people are paying attention. Everyone wants to talk now, she thought. Why not Sunday morning? Where was everyone then? Sunday was when her father's friend and fellow inmate, Andre Anderson, called to tell her that her dad was sweating, struggling to breathe and crying out in pain. "You need to call them and tell them to get some help for your dad," she said Anderson told her.

When she called, she said the person who answered seemed more interested in which inmate had called

Danielle. "Who called you?" the person asked. Who called is irrelevant, she said she told the person on the other end of the phone. She said the person at the work release center told her that nothing could be done until Monday. But the calls from Anderson and at least three other inmates continued. He needs help. He's getting worse. About three hours after her first phone call to the work release center, her father, the man she'll remember as playful and protective, died.

An official investigation is under way, said Bill Miskell, interim public information officer for the state Department of Corrections. Miskell said McCullough saw a doctor last week and saw a nurse Sunday. He said he couldn't say much more until after the investigation. But that investigation meant that her father's body temporarily belonged to the state, that she couldn't see him until after an autopsy.

Is it really him, she thought? How would we know if we can't see him? What rights do we have? Anderson told her, "I hate to say it like this, but the way your dad died, you wouldn't want to see it. He suffered. They watched him die."

And so, a family grieves. People stop by to comfort each other. They look for a photograph that suitably tells the story of his life. And a 23-year-old daughter with a new baby tries to answer reporters' questions while her own questions mount: Is this what it means to be thought of as someone who doesn't matter? Why wouldn't anyone believe him? Why didn't they call an ambulance? Why did her father have to die days short of his 42nd birthday, begging for his life?

By Mark E. McCormick

Published in his book, Some Were Paupers, *Some Were Kings: Dispatches from Kansas,* 2nd edition (Blue Cedar Press, 2020).

War and Violence

Going Down

For me, the war begins in an elevator. Two boys and I are going out to play outside. Other children are already out. They're playing. They're all new friends. They are new. I am new. I'm eleven. We are all new to this place. The apartment building is new. The elevator. We've never been lifted for so many times a day. We would be faster running. But it's all new. We can't miss the ride. The doors are yellow. We run inside. The inside walls are pink. The buttons are round and numbery and fresh. They want to pop out. There is a mirror. It reflects the pink of the walls and the tops of our heads. We are barely tall enough to see our faces. The youngest boy isn't. He jumps and laughs. With his tongue out. And then we are shaken.

We shake and now we are all jumping. We don't know what's happening. We scream out guesses. Tornado? We don't have them here. Is it broken? Did we break it? It's brand new! The building is brand new. And we are... Is it shaking? Where's my sister? We stretch out our hands. We hold on to the walls. The younger boy is smaller. He bends his knees and is looking up. We look like a spider's web. We look abstract. Or surreal. I can't tell.

I see how their faces turn from laughter to fear. Their faces are white spots on the pink walls. I see the eyes of the taller boy. The brown in the eyes is disappearing. The look becomes stiff. The pupil becomes a deep black hole. The iris is becoming more elaborate. It is stretching and loosening, making an intricate web. Another web. I'm thinking it wants to come out. It wants to eat us or freeze us. I can't tell.

My stomach is twisted. It becomes a ball. Heavy. The pink of the stomach becomes the pink of the walls. Not brown like the eyes. Like the poop. Will I poop? I see it all pink, like in my encyclopedia. But the intestines are not neatly going down. Like in the picture. They are scrambled now. Like the eggs my mother makes. But not yellow like the doors. They're pink, like the pink of the walls. Not yellow like the pee. I think I will pee.

We stop now. We are stopped. We are alive. The web undoes. We are not a frozen painting. We are not a scream. We are not abstract.

We go out. The other children are out. They are lying down on the ground. My sister is under a car. A red car. She crawled under. There is a red spot above her eye. She is not all red. She is not bloody. It's just a scratch. The windows are broken. The parents are out screaming. Mom is calling our names. They are alive. Everyone looks confused. The fear is big. I look at them. The iris from the boy's eyes is now upon all of us. It is hugging us. Or clogging us. I can't tell. An hour passes. It was a detonation blast. First one. You don't die from detonations. Unless you're too close. Windows break. Glass falls. Elevators shake. Buildings shake. Yellow and pink become black. They die in a well of the black of the pupil of a child. They fall. I fall. They break. The war breaks. It's how it starts. In an elevator that is going down, that is downing you, not lifting you, that is shaking you, that is making you abstract, abstracting you, enveloping you in an iris of the frightened look, freezing you, breaking you, pink by pink, blast by blast, death by death, day by day. The war for me begins in an elevator.

By Aida Dziho-Sator, PhD, Mostar, Bosnia and Herzegovina

Yes the Killers

like a flock of brilliant birds and so
I wrote that poem he says and I say When

was it that you saw them and he says Four years
ago the day after they found that

missing girl's body in the frozen field
over which I saw them floating and I just had this

feeling you know and I say Yes I know I saw them too
just yesterday all yellow and red and blue all

bunched together still like some small hand
had blossomed just a moment ago and set them free

they were headed north it was a sign to me of things to come
though the trees were all still bare armed

and so sorrowful there It would be nice
he says if we could all be like balloons Yes I say opening

out my hand it would be nice My name is Blue I add
My name is Red he says I search the sky

on the way back home but all around me is that
field there is no moon and the bone chill night is murderous black

like it must have been four years ago and yet somewhere
on the other side of the world it's greening

spring and someone's found little girl lets go a
flock of many colors into the bright beamed face of God

runs laughing open armed towards laughing opening arms and so
I write this poem *Madonna And Child, Laughing* for

Red and me the missing nameless all of us yes the
killers too because I just have this feeling you know if you ever see

balloons

By Robert L. Dean, Jr.
(First appeared in *Illya's Honey*)

Newtown, Connecticut

(After the Newtown school massacre on December 14, 2012)

No words ease the crushing pain.
I don't know the victims.
Never heard of the town.
But those faces,
the front toothless smiles
the tousled hair
their names,
Dylan, Olivia, Chase, Madeleine,
their ages
6, 6, 7, 6
the teachers
the mother
the killer.
I cry for innocent
children, who yesterday
played tag and climbed trees.
I cry for devoted teachers
who spread their wings in vain.
I cry for the worried mother
who tried to help her tormented son.
I cry for the tormented young man
who exploded with hate and senselessness.
I cry for our nation.
I cry for humanity.
I cry.

By Judy Keller Hatteberg

The Quandary

What bothered me most was the noise. And the smoking. And the cold. And the quandary.

Back at the base I'd had a quiet room with one sedate roommate. Aziz liked to play pool, so he was in the common room a lot, and although he smoked, he was a good sort and kept that in the common room as well, since he knew it made me turn green.

In return, I pretended not to notice him praying in his off hours. We had real bunks and kerosene heaters in the barracks to keep us warm, and I never thought much about serious matters like quandaries.

Those were the days when I was a supply manager. The most demanding thing I had to do was get up from my desk and walk back to the stockroom to take inventory. Bootlaces, check. Canteens, check. Helmets, check. It was boring, but at least it allowed me to postpone telling my father that I wasn't going to join him at the mattress shop; that I was going to sell sewing notions with my mother's brother who was rich and whom he hated. So I ordered supplies, hung out with Aziz, and bided my time.

Then the rebels moved closer to the city, and the army was already spread so thin they were forced to call up the likes of us. We had 48 hours notice. I went home to see my parents and my neighbor Amira, who didn't know about my plans to marry her after I'd saved enough from selling safety pins. When I came back everyone's duffel was packed, the supplies had all been shipped to some other base, and Aziz had shot himself. His note was written in quick chicken scratch: "I will not be a killing tool for this malignant regime.

I bear witness that there is no God but Allah and Muhammad is His messenger." I had always admired Aziz for risking his hide by praying; I could never have done something like that. I hadn't really prayed since I was young, except at the Friday prayer. It always burned me that my father said all his prayers faithfully, but it didn't seem to make him any less a miser or brighten the surly scowl he always had for me and my mom. In any case, I began praying in Aziz's place. Silently, secretly (most often with furtive tayammum instead of wudhu), I picked up his habit for him.

The auto repair shop we took over and used as a base camp on the outskirts of Dayraya was cold and damp. There were no cozy diesel heaters or chestnuts to roast on them. Only two harsh, noisy space heaters that were at the mercy of the anemic power grid. Of course our two officers, who stayed in the family's three bedroom house above the shop, had diesel heaters.

They even had diesel, though I have no idea where they got it.

The army told us when we deployed that we wouldn't see any action. Of course if they really believed that, they wouldn't have deployed us--we were the bottom of the barrel. Soft and lazy and expendable. Even our officers were fat and stupid.

Most of the people on the block we held--rebels and civilians alike--had "evacuated;" not really at the point of our guns, but at the sound of our boots anyway. Soon the rebels were fighting their way back toward us, though, as if their leaving had been a mere feint. They knew the streets, and we began to lose men to snipers. I hadn't really been close to any of them. I made it a policy not to get close to anyone after Aziz.

There were no dormitory rooms at the auto shop. All fourteen of us slept, ate, played cards, and roughhoused in the garage. The smoky din made me nauseous. The nausea made me anxious. The anxiety made me nauseous. I spent a lot of time on volunteer watch duty outside, where it was colder and damper but quieter and cleaner.

When I was outside I had to decide between pacing, which made the blisters on my cold feet burst and bleed, or standing still, which invited the cold into my soul. I would sit on the curb and rock back and forth, pretending I was just shivering when I was really saying Aziz's prayers for him. After a while, I began to think of them as my prayers. I began to pray about him rather than in place of him. I began to pray for myself, too. Before, I would occasionally pray for Amira and that was about it.

The more I prayed, the worse I felt. At night I would cover my head to keep out the smell of stale Al Hamras and the sound of guys cheating at Rens. While I fought for sleep, my brain fought back with accusations. I knew the "rebels" were really my classmates and friends. I knew that if I hadn't already been in the army when the war started, I would be fighting alongside them. I would be, wouldn't I? Would I have had the guts to fight, if I'd had the choice? I certainly hadn't had the guts to disobey the order to deploy. Look at me--carrying a Kalishnikov past someone's barber shop in my clunky boots.

Then there was Aziz. Had he been noble to take himself out of the hands of the regime, or had he just taken the easy way out-- preferring an easy death to the torture they would have laid on him if he'd refused to serve? And what about me? Talk about easy ways out. I had told myself that my piddly little job wasn't harming anyone, but supply management is what kept the army marching on neighborhood after neighborhood. It was no different than pulling the trigger myself.

And that always brought me to the quandary: What would I do when it came down to it-- when the choice really was to pull the trigger or not?

I wanted to be strong and refuse to shoot at the freedom fighters, but I didn't want to die. I wanted to stand firm, but I wasn't brave or steadfast or even indignant enough to overcome my own fear. So I kept watch in the cold and prayed I wouldn't have to.

When the quandary came for me I was in the middle of Asr prayer, taking shelter from a drizzly, miserable rain under the overhang behind the mechanic's shop. There was a skullcracking burst of close machine-gun fire, the echoes sucked up immediately into the mist, and then silence. Then the guys began gathering their weapons and slamming on their helmets. The officers came clomping down the stairs and began shouting orders. I thought I was going to avoid my reckoning--that I would be able to hide in the back and get lost in the chaos and not have to meet my true self, whoever he was.

But the officers brought the platoon out the back, and before I knew it I was a real soldier. My helmet was inside, but someone shoved a weapon into my hands and I was carried along with their momentum out into the street. "I didn't finish my prayer . . ." I thought.

We fanned out and took up posts in the doorways of shops, around corners and behind the few cars that had, for whatever reason, not escaped with their owners. I found myself on a small side street, accompanied by Colonel Bayazid. He was shouting orders but I couldn't hear him. I flattened myself against the wall and waited for it to all go away.

When a rebel fell in the street not fifteen feet from me, I began to hear again. He was wearing a red and blue plaid shirt and no coat. There was a set of prayer beads wrapped around his wrist. "There is no God but Allah," he shouted, and tried to bring his pistol up. He saw me. He was struggling to aim.

"Finish him!" shouted the Colonel. He was shooting in the other direction. "Finish him and come cover me!"

And that's when the quandary melted away. There was noise all around, and cold and smoke and chaos, but I was suddenly granted what I had been longing for: peace.

Peace of heart, peace of mind; peace that bloomed from the inside and couldn't be touched no matter what happened on the outside. Absolute tranquility about my own soul, about the fate of my family and my country and the girl I had wished to marry.

I brought my firearm up, pivoted on my heel and shot the Colonel, then rounded the corner and ran to the brother on the ground. He'd been hit in the shoulder and was still trying to aim his pistol at me with his fumbling arm. I tucked the gun into the back of my waistband and began to drag him across the street to his friends.

La illaha il Allah, Muhammad arRasoolullah, I panted over and over. The wounded man's comrades were holding out their arms, waving us in to safety. With about two meters to go I slipped and fell backward. As I struggled to get up, a bullet from one of my platoon members found my uncovered head. I didn't feel a thing.

Except the peace. It stays with me, fills me fully, and shines from me now. I've seen the brother I tried to save a couple of times, although I haven't seen Aziz. I don't know if he is here or not. But it's quiet here, thank God, with clean, crisp air, warm sunshine, and not a quandary in sight.

By Najiyah Maxfield

SOLDIER'S CHRISTMAS

On December 23--he remembers--
G2 detected a Viet Cong battalion
staging a night river crossing.
The 511th popped flares
and cut them to pieces
with M-60s, artillery and Cobras.
The next day they fished
black-clad bodies from sullied waters,
stretched them in rows.
It was the only way they had
to keep score.

The pall of their work
clung to them like smoke
in the vacuum of the Christmas Day
cease fire. Making their way
to the mess hall,
they sat down in rows
to canned turkey, cranberry juice
and Red Cross ditty bags
beside each plate. The chaplain
offered a prayer and then
led them in singing "Silent Night."
The words hung in their throats
like a bayonet's edge,
carving a moment's bridge
to that distant world

of red Santas, church candles
and hearth.

He sits today beside a festooned tree,
grandchildren laughing
among ribbons and wrappings,
their eyes like captured stars.
He listens as the anchor on CNN
drones of the Middle East and war
while young faces beneath helmets
drift across the screen.
He stares then past the tinseled twigs,
past the strung lights to distant shadows.
And there he sees the faces
and hears the rough carol
of the men of the 511th.
And he knows what all young soldiers
will learn--on the long road back
to the sanctity of home
the body count commingles with grace.

By Mark Scheel

Published in *Star Chaser* (Anamcara Press, 2020).

"Soldier's Christmas" appeared in *The Kansas City Star's* Poet's Corner

Carnage

Idrish Ahmed didn't know what had happened. Not until the pain arrived to clue him in. Only then did he process what had befallen him — and what would befall him next. A wave of nausea rolled through, and suddenly...his heart was in Mosul.

It was the last time he'd gone on vacation with his family. 1999, before the fall of the government. He didn't wonder why that particular memory surfaced. He didn't wonder what it said about him as a person or as a Muslim that he should remember their last holiday instead of something deep or spiritual. He just let the memory drown out the agony.

Leena had been pregnant with Rami then. They'd gone to Mosul to see her family. Idris remembered sand pelting the windshield of the Toyota on the way. He remembered sneezing all the way to Mosul, even though the windows had been rolled up and the AC on. He'd been stuffy when they arrived at Leena's father's house -- couldn't even smell the fish the neighbors were frying. Leena said to be thankful for small miracles.

That night, though, he'd been able to smell her hair, lying beside her in the tiny twin bed she'd slept in as a child. Even though she could have removed her scarf in his company after their engagement, she had almost coyly asked him to wait until their wedding night. Idris had been half happy to be patient and half afraid that she was hiding something. Was she bald? Ali, Leena's dependable, down-to-earth older brother, had assured Idris that he'd be glad he waited. So he had. When he removed her scarf on their wedding night and she let her river of straight, black, coconut-scented hair unfurl to her waist, he had literally basked in the knowledge that this treasure was his alone. Two years later, in her bed, he could smell her hair even through his stuffy nose. Either that or he knew the smell so well he could imagine it as soon as he got near her.

The scent of her inspired him to reach out, and he rubbed her bulging tummy. She turned over and draped one leg across him. Even in the overbearing heat, he welcomed her relaxing into him.

They had picnicked on the banks of the Tigris that week, and had served as picnic food for the mosquitoes. Idris remembered lighting the coals for shish kabob and fanning them to redhot with a straw fan he'd bought at Al Shorjah Souk back in Baghdad. He could almost taste the comforting tang of the grilled meat and the smooth coolness of the yoghurt they'd dipped it in. He pictured Leena laughing as she popped a grilled onion she'd peeled for him into his mouth.

That was the last time he remembered eating grilled onions.

Idris thought of seeing his father-in-law cry that week. His mother-in-law, a portly combination of caretaker and colonel, had died only a year earlier, of breast cancer, and Idris had taken his still-mourning father-in-law to the cemetery to visit her. Idris remembered how uncomfortable he'd felt when he saw the old man's tears — as if a mountain were melting before his eyes. He hadn't known where to look.

The next day he'd gone out with Ali. They'd set up their hookahs in a cozy corner of the neighborhood coffee shop — the one next to the florist. Idris remembered playing backgammon with some of the "uncles." Their opponents were regulars at the café — so regular they were almost a part of the place. Idris only came to Mosul a couple of times a year, and even he knew them all by name. Abu Ziyad, Abu Yusuf, and Abu'l Khayt. Abu Ziyad's oldest son was Ziyad, Abu Yusuf's oldest son was Yusuf, but Abu'l Khayt was a tailor who had never married, so he was called Father of the Thread.

Eventually the conversation had turned to politics. International politics, of course. The safe kind. The men began to banter back and forth about whether the US would attack again. Abu'l Khayt was sure they would. "This son of a dog is a bigger dog than his father was. And revenge is a powerful motivator."

Idris had scoffed. His own naïve words shot back at him as if they had come from the blast he'd just witnessed: "The international community won't allow it. The Arab world won't allow it. The Americans know better."

Abu Yusuf had shaken his head. The old men had lived through coups, world wars, and the Revolutionary Guard. They knew better. They knew history. They knew human nature. And they knew the luck of their country.

Idris Ahmed remembered praying the Friday prayer in Mosul that week. The imam was an old classmate of Leena's who'd lost his father and his sister in the war. He talked about the responsibility of raising children. Everyone in the country was worried about their children's physical needs, he lamented, to the detriment of their spirits. People were so worried about getting their kids' teeth fixed, their shoes repaired, and their bellies full that there was no time or energy left for nourishing their souls.

The imam had acknowledged that the country was undergoing a big test, but told them to be grateful they were tested in this manner instead of like the poor, misled Saudis and Kuwaitis — people whose test was wealth and leisure. The Prophet — peace be upon him — had said that wealth was what he feared most for his community. The imam assured the assembled that they were the most blessed in the world. Along with the Palestinians, the Chechens, and the Kashmiris, they formed an elite club of those whom Allah loved enough to test with trials like those of the first Muslims: war and oppression and privation. Yes, they were in good company.

Idris remembered wondering how he would be able to provide for his new family either physically or spiritually. The responsibility was so heavy it bent his shoulders – all the way to the prayer carpet. He remembered sending up an urgent plea that God would send him the strength and wisdom it would take.

After the sermon, he'd found enough courage to ask Ali for a loan. He cringed at the salty disgrace of putting himself in the position of the lower hand, but the one-room flat he and Leena were renting would soon be too small for the Ahmed family, and it was time to build on the land his father had left him. Despite his best efforts, Idris hadn't saved enough to begin yet, so he had to find other means.

His brother-in-law, tall with a broad beard and a smile to match, had been great about it, not rubbing Idris' nose in it either then or later. Of course his wife Jumanah had known about it, though, and that meant that the whole rest of the family found out, too.

Idris smiled, remembering the day he'd paid back the last of the loan six years later, when Rami was five and they'd lived in their new home for four years. He had immediately felt the morbid weight of debt lift off his heart, and had become closer to his brother-in-law, now that they were back on an equal footing. Talking to Jumanah still tripped his gag reflex, though.

Idris wondered what their home looked like now. He pictured it before it had fallen victim to the Americans' peculiar form of liberation. He saw Leena watering her plants, Rami coming up the stairs, back from Qur'an class. But then the bunker buster had come to visit, and they'd had to move in with his sister and her family. Amira's family had welcomed them with open arms, but the stress of living in cramped quarters was taking its toll on everyone.

Something bright flashed near him and jolted Idris back to the present. He was bombarded with the violent sounds of the blast's aftermath — sirens and shouting and scraping metal. He remembered that he had gone to the market to see what half dead vegetables might be available for Leena and Amira to make some sort of nameless stew from. He had just bought a half a kilo of potatoes and a wilted bunch of cilantro when the blast hit.

When he was able to focus on the flashing light, he found it was a camera, wielded by a silent young female reporter. He wondered what she was doing in a war zone if she didn't have to be there.

The woman focused her camera on the poor man — on his body and his severed leg several feet away. She snapped her shutter as he raised his right index finger and spoke something she couldn't make out. Then, without trumpet or fanfare, Idris was reduced to just another bit of carnage.

By Najiyah Maxfield

COMING HOME FROM IRAQ

Have you noticed, the way steel encases flesh,
body armor or casket—the same?

Coming back to the black hole in a city
where it all began.

Twelve thousand miles round-trip
to transport sand to the undertaker.

The moon sits behind the oak branch
like a spider peering down from a web.

Do you hear the cat pawing litter,
covering something up?

A night train clacks toward a crossing,
dissecting the heart with its whistle.

Tomorrow they will bend and touch
the cold, polished marble of death.

By Mark Scheel

Published in *Star Chaser* (Anamcara Press, 2020). "Coming Home from Iraq" appeared in *The Kansas City Star*'s Poet's Corner.

Suicide

Mother's Suicide

(excerpt from memoir *Gun Memories of a Stone Eyed Cold Girl*)

I hear a baby crying. My mother says, "Shush!" My brother, sister, and mother stand in the dark and watch out a window as our father makes his way to the neighbor's house. He is going to steal a loaf of bread because there is nothing in our house to eat. At some point I realize I'm being held by my mother. I am the baby who is crying.

\#

My sister, brother, and I awaken from a deep sleep. We hear a loud sound and run into my parents' bedroom. Our father is standing across the room from my mother. She is doubled over and holding her stomach. His voice is angry as he hollers at us to get into bed. We are frightened, and the three of us run to their bed and climb into it.

\#

My mother is sleeping on the green sofa. She doesn't seem to notice when I rush past her to open the refrigerator and grab an egg from a bowl to take outside where Jena and Scott and I have been playing all afternoon. I will be having my third birthday, so my four-year-old brother and five-year-old sister are making me a birthday cake from mud, sticks, grass, and the egg I just swiped. Scotty digs up a worm and dangles it in front of me. "Eat it! Eat it! Eat it!" they squeal in unison. I refuse. "I will if you do," my brother Scotty promises. "Fraidy cat," my sister taunts. "I am not!" I scream. "It doesn't have ketchup on it." My sister Jena runs into the house and brings back the ketchup in which she smothers the worm. I eat the worm.

\#

I'm caught off guard when my brother says he wants to sword fight with me. I grab the knife laying on the pink translucent plate filled with varied chunks and colors of cheese and our favorite fruits – strawberries, grapes, and bananas – while he runs to the kitchen drawer and grabs a huge wooden-handled butcher's knife. My thumb is quickly sliced open by his larger and more powerful weapon. I run crying in the direction of where my mother lies on the couch with her eyes closed. Her arms are over the top of her head blocking out daylight and the sounds of our play. Her shiny black hair partially obscures her face and is a striking contrast to her porcelain complexion. She is wearing oxford saddle shoes and bobby socks, even though she is lying on the couch. She is dressed in pedal pushers and a blue sweater. It is my sister who comforts me and places a Band-Aid sloppily around my bloodied thumb.

\#

It isn't long before our mother bundles us into our winter coats and sends us outside to play. My brother picks up a handful of bullets lying beside the gun on the coffee table and puts them in the pocket of his red jacket. The gun belongs to my father who is a police officer. We know we aren't supposed to touch it, but we do whenever we think no one is watching.

We run pushing and shoving to the swing set our maternal grandparents have given us. It is our favorite thing to play on. We fight over who gets to swing and who gets to sit on one end of the two-seated glider that goes back and forth fast enough to knock us over if we aren't careful to stay out of its pathway.

We aren't outside long when the snow begins coming down. We try to catch snowflakes on our tongues, but soon, my bare hand touches the metal of the swing set. I begin to cry. I am cold and every part of my body is stinging. My sister runs toward our small white house with red trim to get mittens. The door is locked, and she can't get in.

She peeks through the living room window and says mom has spilled catsup all over herself. We hear a siren in the distance, faintly at first, but it becomes increasingly louder.

\#

We have been playing wildly all evening. Even though we know we shouldn't jump on couches and chairs or run in the house, we do it anyway, and the two women don't say anything to us. They smile sadly and look at each other when we ask when our mommy is coming to get us.

\#

It is dark by the time my father comes to the house. We have been eating crackers and vegetable soup and lots of hot chocolate with tiny marshmallows floating on top. My dad has clothes for us and our pajamas. He takes the three of us outside and tells us to look at the sky. There is nothing to see. It's dark. He tells us to pick one star to look at and that star is now our mother up in heaven. I don't want to look.

I'm cold, and I know my mom isn't a star in the sky. She's at home waiting for us. I'm sleepy and want to go to bed.

\#

My mommy lies in a box at the front of the room. The rest of us are sitting in chairs in rows throughout the church. I want to go to my mommy and wake her up. My uncle carries me to where she sleeps in the box. "Wake up, Mommy! Wake up, Mommy!" I begin to cry and then to scream, "That's not my Mommy! That's not my Mommy!" I am carried out of the room and never see my mom again.

By Ronda Miller

A Child's First Rose

Jill carefully lifted the oven door and let it come to its fully extended position. She removed the two inner grates used for baking the stews her husband he loved. The oven was an older model and the gas knob was still in the on position. With a quick flick of her wrist she turned the green knob. The slow hissing sound grew louder.

With her usual deep sigh of weariness Jill glanced about the kitchen deciding what to do next. She had tried to make her marriage work. As a young couple she and Jim fought a lot about money. But mostly they fought over her drinking. She had hidden bottles away in secret spots which Jim eventually found. His discoveries led to yet another argument and more rounds of accusations. He had scolded her that she was a no-good drunk and an unfit mother. Sometimes she had agreed with him. Now Jim was gone, this time for good he told her. She knew he meant it. Her loneliness crept slowly underneath her skin and was now inside feeding off her like a parasite. In the early days of their marriage she tried to be tolerant of Jim's angry outbursts but her understanding alone was not enough. She knew he had it rough in the Pacific and so made allowances. In his sleep he often moaned about the screeching kamikazes aiming for his ship. Jill had demons of her own which she shared with no one, not even Jim. Her father had also been a drinker. And when Jill began to start blooming into her young womanhood her father began to invite her to have a drink with him alone in his study. In that study her shame grew. More recently her father's whisky breath and rough railroader hands intruded into her thoughts when she least expected it.

Her little boy, Trey, looked on passively watching his mother in the kitchen. He was her oldest son. Today he was wearing his usual holster and toy guns. He loved pretending to be a cowboy and every morning asked his mother to dress him up as one of his western heroes. Usually at this time of day he would be in nursery school, but Jill kept him home today. Jill leaned down to lovingly stroke her son's cheek. "You know I will always love you" she whispered softly. He nodded his head and smiled. She reminded him that "I need you to be my brave little cowboy for mommy today, OK?" He nodded as though he understood. She gave him an affectionate kiss on the forehead and stroked his hair. She then reached into the crib to give his little brother a soothing rub on the back and a kiss on his cheek. His baby brother was playing with a spoon and still had food smeared on his face.

The kitchen chair scrapped loudly across the old linoleum floor as she dragged it to the edge of the opened oven door. It took some extra care for Jill to get the chair positioned exactly the way she needed it to be. She then dragged another table chair and positioned it behind the first one. Together they formed a small bench in front of the oven door. She carefully adjusted the chairs again to get them straight and touching exactly end to end. Satisfied with her progress Jill surveyed the kitchen again. The next step was to seal off all the cracks in the kitchen windows with masking tape and to stuff some old cleaning rags beneath the door to the kitchen. After the rags were carefully stuffed Jill sat calmly on the edge of the chair closest to the oven door. Her breathing was even and measured. In her mind's eye she had seen this image of herself before just as she now sat on the chair at this moment. The mental image she carried had always faded out at this point with her sitting alone in the kitchen. Something had always blocked her from seeing any further. Today she was resolved and could see ahead and knew how the image would end. Almost mechanically she slowly rotated her body to stretch out fully across the chairs, then wiggled and pulled herself head first into the mouth of the black metal interior of the oven. Trey watched his mother lying half in the oven with her hands folded across her chest. "Mommy, why are you doing that?" he asked loud. Jill continued to lie motionless and did not answer her son. The room slowly began to smell of a noxious odor while Trey continued to play with his toy six-shooter as he watched his mother.

The landlady downstairs smelled the odor of the gas and became suspicious enough to call the police. Over the months she had heard the arguments in the apartment overhead and had often debated with herself about what she should do about it. She could tell that something wasn't right with the couple. After the police arrived, she explained that there was a strange odor coming from the rental above and that no one was answering the door. The landlady found the spare key to the apartment and let the officers inside. The odor of the gas was overpowering. The officers made their way to the kitchen and pushed open the door.

****

The policemen let Trey ride in the middle of the front seat of their squad car on the way to the station. He was still wearing his holster with toy pistols and his cowboy hat. He extended his arms and let his tiny hands rest on their shoulders. He talked out loud in a rapid jabber, but they did not respond. In the police station the officers let Trey sit on their desk and play with a stapler while they were busy typing their call reports. One of the secretaries gave him a pile of scrap paper and a stapler he could use to staple together to stay occupied. Then a nice lady in a brown coat arrived and took Trey by the hand. She told him she was from social services and that it was her job to help children like him. He looked at the officers as if to ask if it was all right to leave with the lady. They smiled at him and shook their heads to signal he could go.

****

After a few days the social services lady brought him to a new house and told him he would be staying here for a while. After exchanging a few more words with Trey and his grandmother the social services lady left. He had never met his grandmother before. She wore thick glasses and a yellow flowered apron. His grandmother asked him if he was hungry. He wasn't but accepted a cookie to nibble on. Trey sat with his legs dangling from a chair in the kitchen. He had never seen this place before. He looked about the kitchen but said nothing. The room seemed brightly colored and very clean to him. At the table his grandmother and aunt were talking in hushed tones while occasionally glancing his way. Trey continued to stare down at the top of his shoes. Then slowly his gaze shifted and fell upon the door of the large white oven. The two women talking noticed how he starred wide eyed at the oven door. "He knows doesn't he?" whispered his Aunt in a tone a bit too loudly. "Maybe so. Hard to know, he's so quiet" his grandmother answered. They continued to watch him and talk between themselves. Trey caught only brief snippets of the family discussion throughout the evening as more people arrived. Several times Trey overheard: "what do we do about the boys?" and "where is their father?" No one seemed to have an answer.

****

The grandmother's tiny living room was full of guests wearing suits and Sunday-best dresses. Trey had never seen so many people gathered together before. Some had traveled long distances to be here. Many of the women had very long white hair braided straight back and held with a simple clip. Several introduced themselves as a great grandmother or as an uncle or as a second cousin. They all wanted to talk to Trey and ask him questions. What was his favorite game? How did he like his nursery teacher? Would he be a cowboy when he grew up? Some just wanted to hug him and hold him close. They reminded him that he was getting to be a big boy. One visitor held his hand while gently wiping a tear and told him that everything happens for the best and Jesus loved him. A few brought him a present. One of his aunts from California brought him some sea shells and a collection of minerals that sparkled when he held them up to the light. One of the older uncles was a pilot who belonged to a group of adventurers known as the "High Fliers Club." He had flown around the world in his plane and held Trey on his knee while describing for him the excitement of flying up high in the clouds. One of these days he might take him up in the sky with him so he could see for himself. Trey was enthralled by this uncle's adventure stories and liked this uncle the most among all those in the room who had spoken to him.

****

Trey was seated between his grandmother and his aunt on a wooden church pew. He had never been in a place like this before, so big and with so many bright colors on the windows. The room seemed to overflow with vases of flowers of all kinds, especially with red roses. The fragrance of the roses permeated the air and the sweet smell filled Trey's nostrils. He had never smelled this kind of fragrance before. The pews of the church were soon filled and everyone became quiet as a tall man wearing spectacles and a black robe with a cross on it made his entrance from a small side door. The robed man stood on a small podium and began to speak to the audience in a singsong voice from behind a small, tall wooden table. Trey could only see the robed man from above the shoulders. The man talked for a long time and used big words he did not understand. Trey continued to stare at the many bouquets of flowers and breathe in their rare fragrance. Then the organ started to play and the people stood up to sing some songs from a book they held. Trey heard the phrase about a rock of ages was and wondered what that was.

Rock of Ages, Cleft for me

Let me hide myself in thee

It was hard to sit still and he continued to wiggle in his seat. Finally the man in the back robe was finished speaking and the last of the hymns had been sung. Then the people stood up all together. They made a line and filed slowly past the long, brown metal box that lay on a table at the front of the church surrounded by large wreaths of flowers. Trey had noticed the box earlier in the service but did not know what it was. Some of the people stood and lingered for a long time as they looked inside the special box before moving on. Several wept aloud before turning away. Some needed to be gently held by someone.

It was finally Trey's turn as his grandmother took his hand and walked with him up to the brown metal box. He had not noticed until now that the box had handles on it. His grandmother lifted him up in her arms so he could peek over the edge to see what was inside. No one had told him beforehand what it was he might see. There lay his mother just as he had last seen her, still asleep with her hands folded neatly across her chest. She had changed clothes and was wearing a puffy white dress and her hair was combed back very neatly. He had never seen his mother with red lips and pinkish white cheeks like this before. He thought she was very pretty. The smell of the roses for Trey was now almost overpowering. Trey's grandmother gently asked him if he wanted to give his mother a kiss. He thought about it for a moment and shook his head no. His grandmother seemed perturbed by his answer and asked him again. Many of the people in the church seemed to be watching him, as though anticipating how he would respond to this request. He felt suddenly afraid of being watched and again said he did not want to. He was not sure why, but he felt he was not supposed to kiss her. He had given his mother many kisses before but only when she had been awake. Trey looked away from his mother still asleep in the brown metal box and wriggled out of his grandmother's arms. He could not bring himself to look at her anymore. The church organ started to play again and again Trey wondered about the rock of ages.

Rock of Ages, Cleft for me

Let me hide myself in thee

Finally the organ stopped for good and the people began to file out of the church. Some spoke softly to one another; some hugged and cried. An old lady with streaks of grey in her hair spotted Trey and leaned down to hand him one of the many roses he had seen in the chapel. "This is for you" she said then smiled kindly at him and walked away. Trey's grandmother took him again by the hand and walked with him out through the church doors to the sidewalk by the street. Trey clutched the single rose and walked on with his grandmother into the open air. The sky that day was grey and overcast. It looked like rain.

By George Hough

A Permanent Solution to a Temporary Problem

I met Joe back in 1973 in prison. No, we weren't cell mates serving time. We were volunteers wanting to make a difference. VISTA, acronym for Volunteers In Service To America, was the domestic side of the Peace Corps. We had signed up independently for a year of service as volunteers in Georgia.

At the Georgia Industrial Institute (GII), a.k.a. men's prison, in Alto, GA, our larger team's mission was to set up a pre-release program for inmates approaching their release date. The goal was to help prepare the men to function within the law, and to be successful in the "outside" world without resorting to crime. In other words, to reduce the extremely high rate of recidivism.

We also had a mini-caseload of inmates we counseled.

I've written a poem about Joe who left VISTA and Georgia. Besides his death by suicide, the poem mentions others who were desperate and alone in their final moments.

For people in many careers, handling death comes with the job. These deaths are representative of the mind-numbing investigations I worked as a deputy sheriff.

I never heard a career cop say he or she wanted to work one more death case–whether a fatality wreck, suicide, or homicide. Each one, for sure, sucked a little life-breath out of me, right down to my bone marrow.

Suicide Joe and Buffalo

Lit like a lantern,
Sharp as a knife,
Ready to wrestle,
Eyes so bright.

Wasted and smiling,
Talking of dope.
Wearing a tie,
Looking a joke.

Making changes,
Sacrifices to him.
Others saw it,
As no confirmation.

Unable to take it,
The Pressures of Peer.
Wanting to be seen,
As a young savior.

Stormed out one day,
With his girl and best friend.
Becky and Buffalo,
A part of the blend.

Left behind,
His vest and his tie.
Part of the game,
Part of his try.

Visited him later,
In mid-Illinois.
Showed me his treasures,
Showed me his joy.

I remember the trunk,
And his weapon of war.
The rifle was special,
I remember its bore.

Heard later by letter,
Of Joe's suicide.
Hara-kiri,
Families pride.

Too different than most,
Alike to far few.
Joe left Georgia,
Found death in the truth.

Suicide again,
You heard me right.
One due to cancer,
The other — family fight.

Brawner in the bathroom,
With a twenty-two,
Arlen in the stairwell,
In a dog collar noose.

Uniforms, wakes,
Families in fear.
A lost one, found one,
Children in tears.

Too different than most,
Alike to far few.
Joe left Georgia,
Found death in the truth.

Just a reminder about suicide: most people who are hurting do not want to die, they're looking for a way to stop the pain. Help is available.

If you feel like no one is approachable–not even a friend or family member–then understand, there are toll-free hotlines available.

One number to call is the National Suicide Prevention Lifeline at 1-800-273-8255. They promise this: "We can help prevent suicide. The Lifeline provides 24/7, free and confidential support for people in distress, prevention and crisis resources for you or your loved once.

Remember, suicide is a permanent solution to a (usually) temporary problem. Wait an hour. Wait a day. Ask for help. Ask again. Stick around. You can help yourself and make a difference. Some day you might even write about your trauma and help others who are desperate and in pain.

By Jim Potter

COVID-19 A NOVEL CORONA VIRUS

Someone else said she'd gone to her sister's funeral in Illinois, or maybe it was Indiana.

People watched maple trees bud and mourning doves nest from behind their picture windows. They reread a cozy mystery while restless children stared at iPads. They watched reruns on TV. They tried not to think.

The old woman returned home from Illinois, or maybe it was Indiana, on a Tuesday. She died on Easter morning. They cremated her body.

The preacher prepared a sermon that compared the old woman's life to that of biblical Ruth, a virtuous woman widowed young. He hovered in the pulpit above bouquets and wreaths, the nave redolent with scents of roses and lavender and lilies. Alan Jackson sang traditional hymns, "The Old Rugged Cross" and "Blessed Assurance." The preacher's wife sliced a chocolate cake and brewed coffee for after the service. Chirps of cardinals and robins drifted through doors thrown open to welcome mourners.

Nobody came.

By Michael D. Graves

Virus

Little ones clustered on her porch and wondered. The door cracked open and creaked wide, and aromas of chocolate brownies, or sometimes almond biscuits, or maybe macaroons came from within. A woman in a faded floral housecoat looked down and smiled. The children clapped and yelled and bounced, and little lights flashed on their sneakers. Laughter spilled over the woman's pink gums. She lowered a silver tray, and each child wrapped a tiny fist around a treat as she whispered "dear one" or "sweet angel." They tasted their morsels and looked up and grinned, and she said, "See you tomorrow."

Folks said wasn't it a shame she never had children of her own, what with so much love to share. Widowed young and never remarried, alone all these years. Someone else would say, no, no, that's wrong. She wasn't alone. She had lots of children, and heads would nod.

They closed the school on a Wednesday and sent the children home with notes to their parents. On Friday, they sent the teachers home. The diner closed, and the movie theater, and the bowling alley, and the library. The pharmacy stayed open, and the grocery store, for a few hours each day.

People chatted with each other by phone or on Facebook. They posted pictures of their cat curled on the sofa and the spinach omelet they had for breakfast. Someone said that the old woman's house looked empty and wondered if she was okay. Should someone check on her?

FIST IN THE AIR

Naomi: "How do you know if you are going to die?"

Naomi's mother: "When you can no longer make a fist."

For the past few days
I have had
some symptoms
of something…so this
morning I had a COVID
swab test. I won't know
the results for 5 – 14 days.
By then a person
could be dead.
I got home and opened
my phone to this
beautiful, miraculous
poem of yours.
Thank you.
We must all
continue to make a fist,
raise it high
in the air.

By Michael Poage

Night Quarantine

(Mostar, Bosnia and Herzegovina, May, 2020)

It is three o'clock, the roundest of hours, when night curls itself against the chill and only the faintest pinpricks of light puncture the holy darkness. A scattering of frail and lonely streetlights perform their sentry duty on the bridge beneath my balcony. One apartment shines in this otherwise shuttered apartment building that leans over the river, its occupants hidden and anonymous. I am intrigued by that one small light shimmering against the negation of everything.

In this terrorized world where everyone is afraid of tomorrow, I am not alone.

I make my ghost walk window to window in search of a star, shooting or stable, that might be watching over us. It is two and a half months into quarantine and I have grown strangely contented in my solitude. It tastes of red wine so dry it pulls my mouth. It smells sour, of spring denied its blooms, of April aborted.

The night is silent and chill as the bodies that fill the morgues, the ice rinks, the refrigerated trucks. It is dark and hollow like their coffins, like this city, this night. I want to walk into it, to fill its vacuum with me, feel the river lap my calves and rise to my hips. I want to walk until I am covered, enclosed in its soft shroud that holds at bay the dawn and its questions. Perhaps, if I could reach them without choking for breath, lungs calcified, without suffocation, I would join them, those dead-too-soon. Especially now when dark has arched from mountain to mountain, and lets me stand within its gigantic, impervious sphere.

But I do not move. I don't want to miss the pulling back of the curtain for the last act.

By Gretchen Eick

Published in *The Journal, The Response: Leadership and the COVID-19 crisis*, Special digital edition, dispatch #5 April 6, 2020

The Process of Dying

The Trip

"Let's get out of here and go to Wichita. First, I'll need some foil
to wrap around my feet," she says.
"It smells funny here and I don't know who those people are."
She closes her eyes and leans her head back in morphine haze.
I take her hand in mine. The skin slides too easily
across bones and tendons but her hand is warm.
"We can't go just now," I say "but we will soon."
What else can you say, when you know she has a different trip
to make, and you're helpless to rearrange the itinerary.

Nurse du jour comes out to the screened porch to warn
me not to wear her out, as if my words were strenuous.
Why the hell not, I want to scream. *So she can drift in this haze
three extra days, wondering why there are strangers in her house?*

I want to tell the nurse that we have gathered fossils
in sweetgrass baskets together, read poems aloud in the garden,
counted hawks on fenceposts, and recently, yes recently,
walked the tallgrass prairie one last time.

How can smoothing the sheets, filling the water pitcher, and
measuring your elixir let you know the essence of this person,
and what is good or bad for her? She will slip away from both
of us, just the same. You will feel a small pang, reassure yourself
you did everything you could and go to your next job.

I will sit here in disbelief that it really was true, do a mental inventory of the room where I've loved doing nothing more important than watching dust moats float on lazy summer sunrays. I will sit here until I memorize the shape of the space she used to occupy.

By Linda Gebert

The Only Peace Is a Painful One

Cassie Boone says she doesn't deserve any recognition, any acknowledgment, anything for sitting with a dying 23-year-old man who had just been thrown from his motorcycle.

At first, she asked that I not use her name in this column. "I don't want any appreciation for it," she said through tears. "I couldn't save him. I don't feel like I deserve anything. I don't want people to talk to me about it." She wants the tears to stop, and she wants to share the young man's last words with his mother. "He wanted me to tell his mom that he loved her," she said.

Cassie was driving home from her own mother's house Saturday night on 1-235 when suddenly, traffic slowed. She saw someone standing in the roadway directing cars. Then she saw a motorcycle piled up on the side of the road and a young man, beyond the shoulder, beyond the guardrail, lying on his stomach on a patch of sloping grass. Cassie said she ran to him. She'd taken a CPR class and thought she might be able to help, to comfort and stabilize him until help arrived.

But he was badly wounded, she said, and his legs and back appeared to be broken. She kneeled over him, putting one hand on his neck to take his pulse. She rubbed circles on his back with her other hand. While another motorist called for help, Cassie opened his wallet to figure out his name: Abram Wesley "Wes" Christopher. Born March 12, 1982.

She'd learn later that he went to school in Protection and graduated from Ashland High School in 2000. That he'd earned an associate's degree in liberal arts from Hutchinson Community College and attended Wichita State University. That he was a member of First Christian Church in Protection.

Cassie said she tried to keep Wes calm, but he was in a lot of pain. Then he started shaking. That's when he said, "Tell my mom I love her." "He was just very scared," she said. She continued rubbing circles on his back and, for a moment, he appeared to relax. But she realized that his pulse had slowed. And then it stopped.

When the police arrived, they asked everyone who didn't see the accident to please leave, so she did. But the image of that moment didn't leave her. "I dream about it," said Cassie, 20. "It takes me a long time to go to sleep. I see it when I close my eyes. I get so upset."

Maybe it was because Wes was so close to her age. Maybe because she'd once lost a friend in a motorcycle accident. Maybe it had something to do with her walking away from a nursing career, after completing some of the basic courses, because she didn't think she could stand the sight of blood. "I don't like to talk about it," she said, her tears returning. "I cry whenever I do."

Cassie said her mother suffered right along with her at first, unsure how to help. But then her mother counseled her on how Cassie might try to find Wes' mother and his family. To let them know about the last moments of his life. Cassie tore into the phone book. She called in search of the law officers who worked the accident. She called media. She called funeral homes. But she couldn't find Wes' mother.

And inside, she wondered whether she really wanted

ie Wahto is an institution in Wichita, KS, where she .ught at Butler Community College and organized the area's writers through the Kansas Authors Club, District 5. She writes poetry, including two books, *The Sad Joy of Leaving* (Blue Cedar Press, 2018) and *First, the Reflection* (Spartan Press, 2019), and has edited three editions of a poetry anthology, *365 Days*.

Phil Wood, originally from New England, lived three years in San Antonio, TX, twelve years in Barbados and four years in China, He has been an active member of the Baha'i Faith for nearly sixty years. He presently lives in Hutchinson, Kansas, writes a bi-weekly opinion column for the *Hutchinson News* and serves as treasurer of D-6 Kansas Author's Club.

Note: Not all authors supplied publisher information.

Mark Scheel was formerly an information specialist with the Johnson County Library and a prose editor for *Kansas City Voices* magazine. His 1997 book *A Backward View* was the recipient of the J. Donald Coffin Memorial Book Award. His poetry collection, titled *Star Chaser*, appeared 29 July 2020 from Anamcara Press.

The Reverend Dr. David Stewart, M.D., D.Min, practiced as a family medicine physician for 37 years and co-founded and staffed the Norma Jean Sanders Free Medical Clinic at Kenwood United Church of Christ on the South Side of Chicago. In 2019, he retired from medical practice to serve as Pastor of New Hope United Church of Christ in Glen Rock, Pennsylvania.

Julie Stielstra, erstwhile art history student and lover of animals and birds, divides her time between the Chicago suburbs and rural Kansas. She is the author of two novels, *Pilgrim* (Minerva Rising Press), and *Opulence, Kansas* (Meadowlark Books), and over a dozen published stories. Visit her at juliestielstra.com.

Maaskelah Kimit Thomas, PhD, associate professor at Colorado Technical University and Principal Consultant for Transformative Concepts Consulting Group, has previously published in *Calling the elders: Reclaiming and transforming our communities through elder wisdom* (MotherTongue Cooperative Press), *The Single Mother's Companion: Essays and Stories by Women* (Seal Press) and *I am Beautiful: A Celebration of Women in Their Own Words* (Rose Press).

Najiyah Maxfield is the Editorial Director of Daybreak Press, the publishing arm of www.rabata.org , which promotes positive cultural change through creative educational experiences. Najiyah speaks internationally on Islam and Muslim voices in literature. She lives in Kansas where she kayaks, crochets, and plays "the floor is lava" with her granddaughters.

Cora Poage is a Heart Whisperer specializing in helping her clients quiet their minds, connect with their hearts, and live and lead from Love. Cora believes that aligning with Love individually and collectively, we create Paradise on Earth. Her home is the magical island of Kauai. She travels the world leading retreats, officiating weddings, and exploring sacred sites. Visit her at: https://corapoage.com/.

Michael J Poage has twelve books of poetry published and teaches English literature and language at the University of Dzemal Bijedic in Mostar, Bosnia and Herzegovina half of each year. His most recent books are *Ain't Leavin' This House Rough-Dried* and *An Incident that Might Lead to Something* (Spartan Press, 2020). *Human Ink* won the Nelson Poetry Award in 2016.

Jim Potter is a retired deputy sheriff. He is the author of two books and one play, and currently writes a weekly blog at jimpotterauthor.com. *Cop in the Classroom: Lessons I've Learned, Tales I've Told* is a police memoir. Potter's novel, *Taking Back the Bullet: Trajectories of Self Discovery*, explores the themes of stigma, identity, and self-discovery. The multi-layered stories are an escape into reality.

Jeani Rice-Cranford (they/them) is a writer, pastor, and educator living in rural Tennessee with their wife and their many beloved fur babies. Jeani's interests include public and systematic theology, social activism, and the healing of grief through right-relationship with the Divine, the self, and neighbor.

executive director of The Kansas African American, he is Director of Strategic Communications for the ACLU of Kansas.

Ronda Miller is a Life Coach who works with clients who have lost someone to homicide. Miller is the former state President of Kansas Authors Club (2018-2019). Her books include: *MoonStain, WaterSigns, Winds of Time, and I Love the Child.* https://www.amazon.com/MoonStain-Ronda-Miller/dp/0692434666

Amena Mohamad, Irish-American, earned a BS in Social Work from Wichita State University and attended the University of Sufism in Pope Valley, California for three years. She worked at the Red Cross, Youthville, Annour Islamic School, and a hospital and has traveled to Lebanon, Iran, Syria, and Ireland. She writes about the intricacies of self-development, relationships and the beauty of God in all that is.

Susan Moir. A dyke, an activist and a recovering alcoholic raised in the bounty of the post-world war dreams/nightmares of America's white working class, Susan was educated by liberation movements that brought correction. She spent her life in Boston raising children. reconciling pain and contradictions and striving to be of use in collective struggles for justice.

John Monroe-Cassel, retired, lives in Vermont with his beloved spouse of 40 years, just up the road from their daughter and her family. They also have a rooster and hen couple living in their barn coop. John had a long career in ministry, hospice bereavement care and human sexuality education.

Bill Dee Johnston, widowed after fifty-one-and-a-half years (having lost his dear wife in 2016), lives in Hutchinson, KS with his son, grandson, and two dogs. A retired lab tech, active in the Baha'i faith, he writes poetry and stories.

Mohan Kambampati worked as a geologist in the Geological Survey of India before migrating to the United States of America. Since 1983, Wichita has been home for him, his wife, and two sons. Mohan directed the Wichita Indochinese Center since 1992 and taught at Butler County Community College and Friends University. His 2020 autobiography is *Music of Existence* (Page Publishing).

Erin Kyna is a globally-recognized transformational teacher, leader, healer, yogi, and certified life coach from Australia. Her soul focus is helping others turn fear into freedom through love and empowerment. On her world travels, she has collected tools, mentoring, techniques, and modalities from spiritual leaders to modern scientists, combining them to serve with a full spectrum of life-changing self-empowerment tools and wisdom.

Ruth Maus of Topeka, Kansas, represented Smith College at the annual Glasscock Intercollegiate Poetry Contest. Her poems have appeared in *Inscape, Grecourt Review, River City Poetry, The Orchards Poetry Journal,* and *Lighten Up Online*. Her book of poetry, *Valentine*, was published in 2019 by Meadowlark Press.

Mark E. McCormick is a journalist and communications professional whose book *Some Were Paupers, Some Were Kings: Dispatches from Kansas* is Wichita State University's 2020-21 campus read. Mark co-wrote *Barry Sanders: Now You See Him: His Story in His Own Words.* Formerly

Michael D. Graves is the author of three novels set in 1930s Wichita: *To Leave a Shadow*, a Kansas Notable Book, *Shadow of Death*, and *All Hallows' Shadows*, all featuring detective Pete Stone. His writing has appeared in *Cheap Detective Stories, Thorny Locust, Flint Hills Review,* and elsewhere.

Judy Keller Hatteberg taught with the Wichita Public Schools for over 30 years. After retirement, she returned to writing poetry and memoirs. Her articles have appeared in several local newspapers. She lives in Wichita, Kansas with her husband, Larry, where she meets with a small weekly poetry group called The Wayward Poets.

George Hough lives in Cambridge England with his wife, Sallye, and his younger daughter, Sage. His older daughter, Chloe, is studying graphic arts in Lawrence, Kansas. He works as a clinical psychologist for the U.S. Air Force and enjoys exploring nature and history in the UK.

Miriam (Miller) Iwashige is a lifelong member of the Amish-Mennonite community near Partridge, Kansas. She and her Japanese husband Hiromi have three married sons and nine grandchildren. Miriam retired from teaching in 2018. She loves nature, and benefits from relationships within her large extended family and faith community and beyond.

Janet Jenkins-Stotts' works have been published in "River City Poetry," "Dash," "Passenger," "Heartland," "The Sea Letter," "Lighten Up Online," "Haibun Today," and "Burningword." She taught at Wichita State U., K.U. and Highland Community College. She now lives in Topeka, KS with her husband, Dave and their miniature pincher, Romeo.

The Reverend Dr. Richard Eick served two parishes in metro Washington, DC, and one in rural Iowa, offering pastoral care to the dying and the grieving. He helped shape the hospice movement as a founding Board member of Hospice of Northern Virginia. In retirement, he has been the Visitation Minister for a church in Rochester, Minnesota the home of the Mayo Clinic.

Eyyup Esen, from Turkey, earned his PhD in higher education the University of Kansas, which awarded him Outstanding International Graduate Student in 2014. Through the Dialogue Institute, aka Movement of Global Warming of Hearts, he organizes events to promote peace and dialogue between cultures and ethnicities. His books are *Global Warming of Hearts!* and *I am not color blind.*

Cammie Funston is a native of Wichita, Kansas with a degree in Communication Science and Disorders from Wichita State University. A retired educator, and grandmother of twelve, Cammie enjoys treasure hunting in used bookstores. "Send me on a mission to find beautiful children's books, and I am a happy woman," she says.

Linda Gebert focusses on visual arts–silversmithing, enameling, painting--and also enjoys writing poetry and fiction. Her work life as a graphic designer, technical illustrator, and teacher of silversmithing was enhanced by participating for many years in a women's creative writing group led by poets Anita Skeen and later Jeanine Hathaway.

The Reverend Edward Ernest Goode, a retired United Church of Christ minister and associate conference minister in Chicago, was born and raised in Boston, MA. His has been an urban centered justice seeking ministry. He is not looking forward to September 13 when he will have to muffle "Happy Birthday" to Lewis.

Sharon Hill Cranford, PhD in adult education and family counselling, worked in education and business before co-authoring *Kinship Concealed* (2013) after discovering her Amish roots. Her published children's books are *Charley and the Hornbook* (about the childhood of the main character in Kinship) and *Gramuhn Knows Best* (2020). A community activist, she leads African-Americans Renewing Interest In Spirituals Ensemble (ARISE).

Robert L. Dean, Jr. is the author of *The Aerialist Will not be Performing: ekphrastic poems and short fictions to the art of Steven Schroeder* (Turning Plow Press, 2020), and *At the Lake with Heisenberg* (Spartan Press, 2018). A multiple *Best of the Net* nominee and a *Pushcart* nominee, his work has appeared in fourteen journals.

Aida Džiho-Šator, PhD, is professor of English literature at the Džemal Bijedić University of Mostar, Bosnia and Herzegovina. Her poems have been published in *Castello di Duino Poetry Collection* in Italy, *Balkan Literary Herald*, *Pitchwise*, and the literary magazine *Life*, one the oldest and most acclaimed literary magazines of Bosnia and Herzegovina. She lives with her husband and two children in Mostar.

Gretchen Eick, PhD, is a social change scholar--*Dissent in Wichita: The Civil Rights Movement in the Midwest* (University of Illinois, 2007) and *They Met at Wounded Knee: The Eastmans' Story* (University of Nevada, 2020). Her novels are *Maybe Crossings, Finding Duncan, The Hard Verge: Britain, 2025* and *The Set Up, 1984: Classified until 2064* (Blue Cedar Press, 2020).

About the Authors

Donald Betts, Jr., formerly Kansas's youngest State Senator and candidate for U.S. Congress, is Monash University's first African American Juris Doctorate. Betts is a lawyer at the global law firm Norton Rose Fulbright in Australia, working with Jaramer Legal, Australia's first national Indigenous law firm. A commentator for Australian news outlets and co-host of 'Greenland the Podcast' (www.greenlandthepodcast.com), he explores differences and similarities between the United States and Australia.

Julie Ann Baker Brin works for public broadcasting and participates in creative and community-building endeavors. Her writing has recently been presented by Wichita's *River City Poetry*, in the 2019 and 2018 *Kansas's Best Emerging Poets* collections by Z Publishing, and in other Sunflower State publications like *Archaeopteryx, Coelacanth, and Sheridan Edwards Review* (in which she received a Kisner Prize for Poetry).

Death is inevitable. How we relate to it is our choice. When I die, I would love for there to be a giant party with music, dancing, celebration, tears, laughter, and star gazing. I would love for everyone to look up in the sky and see me twinkling as part of the Universe. Returned to Infinite Expression. No longer a Bridge, but finally, and forever Home.

By Cora Poage

When I was two weeks old, I stopped breathing. A quick thinking and intuitive nurse saved my life. Through healing sessions as an adult, I realized that I had tried to go "Home". I remember moving towards a window of Light. And wanting to go back through. I heard a beautiful deep voice say, "Not now, honey. I am so sorry but it is too soon. You need to go back and be A Bridge from Heaven to Earth, and Earth to Heaven."

So I came back into my body, and here I am. But I now have an imprint within me of the afterlife. We are all Bridges from Heaven to Earth, and Earth to Heaven. We are all connected to this world and the after-world. We can all remember the Limitless Love of Heaven when we choose to tap in. It's one breath away. Close your eyes, and feel it.

Birth and Death are different sides of the same coin. When we are born, we shift from infinite energy to finite form. And when we die, we change from finite form, to infinite energy. So really, Death is Freedom. It is the invitation back to Infinite Love.

Through my Intuitive Coaching work, I connect to many souls who have passed on from their bodies, and they ALL are laughing with glee. "I'm free!! I'm not stuck and contained in a body. I know you are all sad and missing me, but please know that I am amazing!"

What if we chose to celebrate Death as a way that our loved ones (and someday ourselves) will experience the deepest level of Freedom and Love available to us? What if in the midst of our grieving the human form, we could experience profound joy for the one who has passed and what they are now experiencing?

Epilogue

Sorrow Kite

(A poem for a grieving child)

The next time you feel sad and blue
And wound up tight here's what to do,
Cry and wail and weep and shout
And let your sorrow kite fly out.

Let her flap and dip and fight
And soar to reach the highest height.
If you need help to launch her right
Ask a friend to share the flight.

Let her pull from deep inside
The tail of sadness you can't hide.
White flags waving in the wind
Surrendered memories ascend.

Release her spindle let her climb
'Til every inch of string unwinds
When sorrow has you tight in tow
Open your hands and let her go.

by Cammie Funston

"Jalalud'din Rumi is one of the world's most revered mystical poets. During his lifetime he produced a prolific range of inspiring and devotional poetry which encapsulates the Sufi's experience of union with the divine.... Although Rumi was a Sufi and a great scholar of the Qu'ran his appeal reaches across religious and social divisions. Even during his lifetime he was noted for his cosmopolitan outlook. His funeral, which lasted 40 days, was attended by Muslims, Jews, Persians, Christians and Greeks.

Rumi was born in 1207 on the Eastern shores of the Persian Empire. He was born in the city of Balkh (in what is now Afghanistan), and finally settled in the town of Konya, in what is now Turkey. It was a period of remarkable social and political turbulence. The 13th Century was the era of the crusades; also the area where Rumi lived was under constant threat of Mongol invasion." From https://www.poetseers.org/the-poetseers/rumi/, *by Tejvan R. Pettinger*

'Where Everything Is Music'

Don't worry about saving these songs!
And if one of our instruments breaks,
it doesn't matter.
We have fallen into the place
where everything is music.
The strumming and the flute notes
rise into the atmosphere,
and even if the whole world's harp
should burn up, there will still be
hidden instruments playing.
So the candle flickers and goes out.
We have a piece of flint, and a spark.
This singing art is sea foam.
The graceful movements come from a pearl
somewhere on the ocean floor.
Poems reach up like spindrift and the edge
of driftwood along the beach, wanting!
They derive
from a slow and powerful root
that we can't see.
Stop the words now.
Open the window in the centre of your chest,
and let the spirits fly in and out.

By Rumi*

Translated by Coleman Barks, published in *From Rumi—Selected Poems* (Penguin Books, 1999).

My Sweet, Crushed Angel

You have not danced so badly, my dear,
Trying to hold hands with the Beautiful One.
You have waltzed with great style,
My sweet, crushed angel,
To have ever neared God's heart at all.
Our Partner is notoriously difficult to follow,
And even His best musicians are not always easy
To hear.
So what if the music has stopped for a while.
So what
If the price of admission to the Divine
Is out of reach tonight.
So what, my dear,
If you do not have the ante to gamble for Real Love.
The mind and the body are famous
For holding the heart ransom,
But Hafiz knows the Beloved's eternal habits.
Have patience,
For He will not be able to resist your longing
For Long.
You have not danced so badly, my dear,
Trying to kiss the Beautiful One.
You have actually waltzed with tremendous style,
O my sweet,
O my sweet crushed angel.

by Hāfiz (1310-1390), a Persian (Iranian)
Translated by Daniel Ladinsky

Letting Go

cook onion soup for you all,
and be the grandma
Heaven could not hold,
the one who couldn't stand
to be so far away.

                                        By Gretchen Eick

Please, can we be Mexican?

> *"like Easter bread in your grandmother's*
> *hands. She'll come back.*
> *heaven having been*
> *too far from home*
> *to hold her. O it will*
> *be beautiful."*
> Gabrielle Calvocoressi's *"At Last the New Arriving"*

Sugar skulls and small skeletons,
familiar 3-D scenes alive
on the wall.
Mexicans let the dead thrive.
They bring food to the grave,
eat, and tell tall stories
of those who've gone before.
Death another part of life.
I don't want death to hide
in hospitals, don't want to
watch undertakers
collect the debris
of abandoned bodies
in black plastic bags
taken out like trash.
I want us to pass on
recipes and laugh at
the eccentricities we
each brought to this life.
Will you build a tableau for me?
I'll live small on your wall,

I will end with this statement by Baha'u'llah. I had this quote in mind when I felt like I was approaching death.

"I have made death a messenger of joy to thee. Wherefore dost thou grieve?"

(Baha'u'llah, Arabic Hidden Words)

By Phil Wood

He continues to explain what happens to the soul after a person dies.

"Know thou of a truth that the soul, after its separation from the body, will continue to progress until it attaineth the presence of God, in a state and condition which neither the revolution of ages and centuries, nor the changes and chances of this world, can alter. It will endure as long as the Kingdom of God, His sovereignty, His dominion and power will endure. It will manifest the signs of God and His attributes and will reveal His loving kindness and bounty."

He continues with this explanation of the soul after the death of the body

"The nature of the soul after death can never be described, nor is it meet and permissible to reveal its whole character to the eyes of men. The Prophets and Messengers of God have been sent down for the sole purpose of guiding mankind to the straight Path of Truth. The purpose underlying Their revelation hath been to educate all men, that they may, at the hour of death, ascend, in the utmost purity and sanctity and with absolute detachment, to the throne of the Most High. The light which these souls radiate is responsible for the progress of the world and the advancement of its peoples."

"The world beyond is as different from this world as this world is different from that of the child while still in the womb of its mother. When the soul attaineth the Presence of God, it will assume the form that best befitteth its immortality and is worthy of its celestial habitation."

the other major religions. I asked several ministers this question. One answer was all religions lead to God, but Jesus was unique, and He was raised from the dead. It did not seem to me that should be the only reason to believe.

Several ministers told me Christianity was the only way and all the other religions were false. I did not believe that either. I gave up on organized religion. My life took a downward turn. I became an alcoholic. I went into the army. I started living with a married woman who was not my wife. I met a sergeant who said he did not drink alcohol. I thought this very unusual for an army Sergeant. I asked him why he did not use alcohol. He said it was against his religion. So, I asked him about his religion. He said he was a Baha'i. I studied the Baha'i teachings for about a year and joined the Baha'i Faith in 1962. The Baha'i teachings answered all my questions.

Before talking about death, it is necessary to learn about the soul with this quote from the teachings of Baha'u'llah,

"Thou hast asked Me concerning the nature of the soul. Know, verily, that the soul is a sign of God, a heavenly gem whose reality the most learned of men hath failed to grasp, and whose mystery no mind, however acute, can ever hope to unravel. It is the first among all created things to declare the excellence of its Creator, the first to recognize His glory, to cleave to His truth, and to bow down in adoration before Him. If it be faithful to God, it will reflect His light, and will, eventually, return unto Him." (Baha'u'llah, Gleanings, p. 158)

Baha'i Teachings on Death

Several years ago, I served as a volunteer with a medical team which went to a very remote hospital in Honduras. Near the end of my two weeks stay at the hospital I contracted malaria. The next day we flew to La Ceiba. I immediately went to my hotel room and went to bed with a fever of 105 degrees F. I felt very weak and just wanted to die. I began to have this wonderful vision of floating upwards towards dense white clouds. As I approached the cloud, I could see an opening. Through the opening I could see a beautiful meadow with a stream running through it and a lovely grove of trees. I felt like I was going home. I continue to float upward to go through the opening. As I was about to go through the opening to this beautiful meadow, I heard a loud voice say, "NOT NOW" and the opening closed.

I had the feeling that I had been going to my heavenly home and had I been able to go through the opening I would have died. I was disappointed and I continued to feel like I wanted to die. I started to sweat profusely and within a short time my fever broke, and I started to feel like I wanted to live. I do not know if this was a near death experience. But I felt like I came very close to dying. The next day my friends helped me to get on the plane and through the trip to my home in Hutchinson.

I was baptized as a Christian when I was a baby. I went to Sunday school and became a member of the youth group. I joined the church when I was in high school. When I went to college, I began questioning my belief in Christianity. I wondered about the relationship between Christianity and

We have come because the time of death of a loved one is one of those sacred opportunities in life when we know that life is fleeting and truly a gift from God. Thus, it is especially right and proper to come before God to meditate and to pray and to reflect on the true meaning of life.

This is indeed a sacred opportunity ...a consecrated time...Our Lord Jesus has said

"whenever two or three are gathered together in my name, I am in your midst."

The Lord is indeed in our midst. May our worship be in spirit and in truth.

By Richard Eick

WORDS OF GREETING AT A CHRISTIAN FUNERAL

Dear Friends, we are gathered here in this sacred place

+ to give praise to God,

+ to witness to our faith as followers of Christ,

+ to remember the life of_____ (NAME) _____

who was born on ___(date)___ , and who departed this life on ___(date)___ .

But let us remember that we gather here today in worship, not so much for ___(FIRST NAME)___ benefit as for ours.

___(NAME)___ has entered a new relationship with God –(her/his/their) Creator and ours – and we know in faith that (s/he/they) is safely in God's care.

We have come because the time of death is one of those sacred opportunities in life when it is our hallowed duty to tend to the last needs of the mortal body of a loved one

We have come because the time of death is one of those sacred opportunities in life when deep reservoirs of feelings are released and when it is especially necessary and right to come before God and into the company of family and friends to seek help and guidance in coping with those feelings.

1. God is all knowing. Humans are not. Therefore we must accept that we will never fully understand why some things happen.

2. Scripture does not promise no pain or death. It promises that God will be with us, comforting us through all things.

3. When scripture speaks of free will (and it does so, over and over again), it includes more than accepting Jesus Christ as our personal savior. It encompasses personal as well as corporate choices in life. For example, as a nation, we speak reason, fairness and Christianity, while embracing enslavement, racism and greed. When consequences come, more than the perpetrators are impacted. ("Sunshine and rain fall on the just and unjust").

4. Christian life is like learning to drive a car. While there is no guarantee than no one will crash into you, if you read the roadmap (Bible), if you learn and trust the rules of the road (faith), if you obey the safety guidelines (love), God's righteous hand will guide you toward safety, comfort and peace while you're on this earthly journey.

I have kept this road map close, and it helped, when, a year and a half after losing Doc, my mother passed. I will continue to keep it close for future uphill, rocky climbs along life's highway. I pray that it will be a blessing to you.

Blessings.

By: Sharon Hill Cranford, PhD

A ROADMAP TO COMFORT AND PEACE

The avalanche of sudden losses in my family drove my mind back to long forgotten comments by my father (a Methodist minister). From my aunt, to whom I was very close (my father's youngest sibling) to my brother's wife, six months later, to my brother's death, within the year, the pain had my head and heart reeling. Throughout all of this, my husband was battling pancreatic cancer. While trying to work through these devastating trials. I buried myself in community work. I was then hit with the news that my four-and-a-half-year-old grandson succumbed to the head injuries he sustained in a one-car accident. The car was driven by an inattentive relative, which caused our family dynamics to change forever.

Losing one's grandchild is a triple "whammy". First, it is unnatural, unsettling and often unspeakable. Then, there is the pain of suddenly losing such a beautiful, healthy, happy person from your life. And finally, you have to bear witness to the light that goes out of your child's eyes, as he buries his child. That "death walk" of the traditional funeral procession is something I will pray to un-see for the remainder of my days. The loss of my grandson, Collin also caused my husband, "Doc" to give up. After Collin's death, all Doc wanted to talk about was going to see about Collin. Eight months later, he was gone.

But, back to the sage remarks from my father. He said that, in order to appreciate the goodness and comforting nature of our powerful and benevolent God, there are at least four factors that we must consider. Only then can we begin to heal from the gripping pain of losing loved ones.

Quotations:

From Imam Ali Ben Abi Taleb:

"Do for this life as if you live forever, do for the afterlife as if you die tomorrow."

From the Muslim poet Rumi:

- "Goodbyes are only for those who love with their eyes. Because for those who love with heart and soul there is no such thing as separation."

- "Die happily and look forward to taking up a new and better form. Like the sun, only when you set in the west can you rise in the east."

- "Everyone is so afraid of death, but the real sufis just laugh. Nothing tyrannizes their hearts. What strikes the oyster shell does not damage the pearl."

- "I learned that every mortal will taste death. But only some will taste life."

Death in Islam

The two largest groups of Muslims – Shi'a and Sunni-- vary slightly in their traditions but believe that the soul continues to exist after death and that while they are living a person can shape their soul for better or worse, which will affect whether they go to paradise upon their death. Muslims believe there will be a day of judgment by Allah (God).

The eyes of the deceased will be closed and the body washed three times by family or friends and laid out with their arms across their chest and their head facing Mecca. The body is shrouded, meaning it is wrapped in a simple white cloth, then in each of three additional cloths while prayers are said.

The body will be buried within 24 hours. Among some Muslims, women and men attend the burial, but among others, only men are present for the burial, while women pray at the home of the deceased. Funerals do not include a eulogy. Caskets are generally not used and, as in Judaism, bodies are not embalmed. Cremation is prohibited.

Friends bring food to the mourning family during their time of mourning, which varies, for some Muslims only one day, for Arabs usually three days, and for others forty days. Widows should mourn for four months and ten days during which they are expected to stay apart from the public during that time.

The Grief Gap

"Nothing can make up for the absence of someone whom we love, and it would be wrong to try to find a substitute; we must simply hold out and see it through. That sounds very hard at first, but at the same time it is a great consolation, for the gap, as long as it remains unfilled, preserves the bonds between us. It is nonsense to say that God fills the gap; God does not fill it, but on the contrary, the Lord keeps it empty, and so helps us to keep alive our former communion with each other, even at the cost of pain."

by German theologian Dietrich Bonhoeffer*
from his book *Letters and Papers from Prison.*

Bonhoeffer was executed by the Nazis on April 9, 1945 for his participation in a plot to kill Hitler.

Submitted by Richard Eick

Between loving and dying
Because both are holding the entire magnificence of existence
In my heart
So in order to love more
I allow things to die
And witness it not as a death
But as the perfect, unfolding miracle
of more love

                                                by Erin Kyna

between living and dying

I'm stuck in the duality again
Between the perfection and the pain
I introvert and find god
And upon meeting, god says
Isn't it all just so beautiful
And I reply, as always
It is
I turn outwards again and struggle
I see his pain,
And hers,
And mine.
Inward I see the flames that fuel
but outwards, those flames destroy
I find myself, what,
Grasping
Because of the lie that love is scarce
Fooled into believing
The life long lie
That I'm too difficult to love
So god sent some teachers
To say, have you learnt this yet?
How long will you stay,
When you give more than you receive?
Will you live the old story or the new?
I'm not staying god
I'm free falling
I'm surrendering into you
I'm accepting the perfection of the pain
Because I know that you're smashing me open
I cannot see the difference

From *The Soul of the Indian*

"He [the Native American] is never permitted to forget that he does not live to himself alone, but to his tribe and his clan. . . .

We believed that the spirit pervades all creation and that every creature possesses a soul in some degree, although not necessarily a soul conscious of itself . . .

[Indians] saw miracles on every hand—the miracle of life in seed and egg, the miracle of death in lightning flash and in the swelling of the deep! . . .

The virgin birth would appear to him scarcely more miraculous than is the birth of every child that comes into the world, or the miracle of the loaves and fishes excite more wonder than the harvest that springs from a single ear of corn."

by Dr. Charles Ohiyesa Eastman (1858-1939)*

Eastman was a Dakota physician who fled to Canada in late 1862 with his grandmother following his people's war against the United States. They lived as refugees there until his father found him and brought him to live in Flandreau, South Dakota. His father sent him to college and medical school in the East. Eastman was a life-long advocate for indigenous Americans, wrote eleven books, lobbied Congress, and worked for the YMCA and the Indian Bureau of the U.S. Interior Department.

A Silent Gathering

At the grave side service,
we stand quietly
on a windy Saturday afternoon.

They lift the red, white, and blue cloth
from the casket and fold it
slowly, tenderly,
until we see
a perfect blue triangle with white stars.

No small talk or cell phones
distract us
from the flag folding ritual
of this honorable veteran.

The only sounds and motions
are the swaying prairie grasses
and the fluttering cottonwood leaves.

The unhurried ceremony
provides a respite
from our insane collective busyness.

We have time to reflect on
our own lives and destinies...

who we are
and why we are
and what we could be.

by Judy Keller Hatteberg

grieving family invite their extended family members and friends for a culmination feast. The twelve-day mourning period isolates the grieving family from the community, and it has a practical reason. If the deceased had an infectious disease, the twelve-day isolation is meant to stop its spread.

Hindus believe that although the physical body dies, the individual soul may pass on to another existence through reincarnation, depending on one's karma (the consequences of one's actions over one's lifetime). This is the central premise of death and reincarnation in Hinduism. Of course, knowing this will not give much consolation when those near and dear pass away.

Those of the Hindu faith prefer to die at home, surrounded by family. After cremation the ashes are normally immersed in sacred body of water or ocean.

Some people question why death is always portrayed as dark and sinister? The Sadhguru of Isha answers, "If we look at how we have perceived and portrayed death in India, you will see that death is not seen as sinister. The dark thing about death is the loss for the living. If people lose something precious to them – it could be things; it could be people – they will break down.

So, it is darkness only for the living, but death itself has always been portrayed as a grand event in this culture."

By Mohan Kambampati

CONCEPT OF DEATH AMONG HINDUS

In India if a person is seriously ill the immediate family's concern is getting appropriate treatment for that person's recovery. Meanwhile the close family members, if they are out of town, will be informed about the situation. If the attending physician informs them that survival of that patient is only a remote possibility and it is only a matter of time until he/she is likely to die, only then are any funeral arrangements made.

Hindus traditionally cremate their dead for swifter, more complete release of the soul. The body is seen as a prison for the soul, one that generates attachments and desires that prevent progress of the soul towards freedom. Therefore, in Hindu funerals, the role of cremation is to sever the ties of the soul to the body that it is leaving, freeing it to more toward liberation or emancipation. Cremation should happen soon after death so that the deceased's attachment to the earth and its people is does not become too strong before they are released.

Hindu death rituals in all Indian traditions follow a fairly uniform pattern drawn from the Vedas. However, funeral service rituals vary between sects and subsects, region, caste and family traditions.

One of the Hindu customs dictates that when someone in the immediate family dies, living family members should not visit any one for twelve days. On the twelfth day, rituals are performed for the peace of the dead by a priest. At that time, Hindu priests read scriptures and declare the end of formal mourning. Then visiting can resume. On the twelfth day, the

Children looked on and learned about caring for each other when death visits. Hymns filled the air as the crowd softly sang along with the appointed singers. Mourners huddled shoulder to shoulder to break the force of the stiff and hot south Kansas wind to keep dust from blowing into the eyes of the family members seated downwind in the shade of a tent. Passing traffic droned and roared by turns. When the nearby cross-country highway was built, it turned aside for the cemetery, but the traffic noise intrudes nonetheless. The pastor's voice rose above it all. "Dust to dust, ashes to ashes. . . the spirit has returned to God who gave it. . . death is swallowed up in victory. . ."

"Does death get any better than this?" one speaker asked during Mary Martha's funeral.

After the burial of this saint was complete, we could all answer with a resounding "No."

By Miriam Iwashige

I remember that when I was an adolescent and Mary Martha taught our Sunday School class, she asked us one day if we knew the song "How Beautiful Heaven Must Be." Shy in the presence of our peers, none of us admitted to knowing the song, so she proceeded to sing it for us. I thought of her singing yesterday and reflected on the fact that she had been anticipating for many decades the beauty she is enjoying now.

All these happy reminiscences and bright thoughts of heaven collide cruelly however with the earthy realities of needing to dispose properly of a dead body when someone dies. I understand why in many cases a casket stays safely perched over an open grave till the crowd disperses and the heavy equipment can be brought in. But I like the way Mary Martha was buried, and I hope our way of burial never changes.

Mary Martha's grandsons were pallbearers. They helped some of the brothers from the church carefully lower the casket into the hole in the ground beside her mother's grave. Then, as carefully as husky young men are capable of, shovelful by shovelful, the cavity was filled in around the edges of the casket. And then the parade of assistants began to step forward to relieve the pallbearers. One by one they took a shovel and helped to tuck into the earth Mary Martha's worn-out body. Sons, granddaughters, pastors, nephews, nieces, friends, even a very small great grandson who noticed a few clods that rolled off the mound when the job was nearly finished and picked them up carefully and tossed them onto the pile--no one labored sad and alone, or hurriedly and mechanically to finish the task.

How to Bury a Saint

Yesterday I attended the funeral of Mary Martha, who has been part of our church community for 88 years. Her seven children, 40 of her 46 grandchildren, and all but eight of her 33 great grandchildren gathered to bid their final goodbye, along with hundreds of friends and relatives. One of her sons came from Romania for the funeral and a daughter came from El Salvador. A grandson in Thailand and one in Bangladesh were unable to attend.

She lived in the tradition of the Biblical sisters Mary and Martha--like Martha, cooking generous and tasty meals for housefuls of company, and like Mary, putting aside her duties regularly to fellowship with her Lord.

One of her sons, when he was a child on his way to the bathroom at four o'clock in the morning, found her sitting at her sewing machine. She wasn't sewing. "Mama, what are you doing?" he asked.

"I'm praying," she answered.

"Why are you praying?"

"Because I have five boys and I don't know how to raise them. I'm asking God to show me." she replied. Now, nearly 50 years later, it's clear that she heard from God and followed up on what she learned. Three of her children work full time in Christian ministries. Another son is a pastor in our church. All her children are faithful Christians.

Don't worry dear.
Your secret is safe with us.

How natural you look this evening.

By Robert L. Dean, Jr.
(First published in *Red River Review*)

The Viewing

Lifelike.
What you always wanted to be.

Formaldehyde
so much more permanent

than blood.
No more

heart murmurs
to keep you awake nights

wondering
what we will make of it when you're gone.

That phial of white beach stuff on the mantelpiece.
On what island

did you open yourself up
so much that it hurt.

Under which moon
did you pluck those ten thousand

god-grains from
naked flesh,

casket that one fleeting moment of
perfect penetration.

Shiva often ends with a walk around the block. This can tenderly symbolize mourners' slow reentry into the outside world. Friends and family can accompany mourners on this walk as a show of support. Jewish tradition recognizes that grief continues long after shiva and offers additional rituals to support mourners beyond this initial period of grief.

The Mourners' Kaddish—The *Kaddish* is recited by the mourners for the first time at graveside. Traditionally, it is recited every day for 11 months following burial and then on the *yahrzeit* (yearly anniversary) of the deceased.

Exalted and hallowed be God's great name in the world which God created, according to plan.
May God's majesty be revealed in the days of our lifetime and the life of all Israel — speedily, imminently, To which we say: **Amen.**
Blessed be God's great name to all eternity.
Blessed, praised, honored, exalted, extolled, glorified, adored, and lauded be the name of the Holy Blessed One, beyond all earthly words and songs of blessing, praise, and comfort.
To which we say: **Amen.**
May there be abundant peace from heaven, and life, for us and all Israel.
To which we say: **Amen.**
May the One who creates harmony on high, bring peace to us and to all Israel.
To which we say: **Amen.**

Adapted from https://reformjudaism.org/practice/lifecycle-and-rituals/death-mourning/

as the mourners pass in between, the following words are recited: - May God console you with all who mourn in the midst of the Gates of Zion and Jerusalem." Participants then proceed to the house of mourning to participate in the shiva.

Beginning with the family's arrival at home after burial, a process begins that leads the bereaved gently but firmly back to life and the world of the living. After washing their hands before entering the deceased's home, the family enters and a member of the family generally lights a shiva candle, which generally is provided by the funeral home and which will burn for seven days.

Generally, mourners do not leave the home during shiva. Nor are they to shave, use makeup, or attempt to "look their best." The custom of covering mirrors implicitly conveys to the griefstricken individual that personal appearance simply does not matter now. In doing so, it tacitly removes any cause for embarrassment that mourners might feel.

The first stage in this gradual process of healing is called shiva. The period of shiva is intended to see parents, sibling, child, and spouse through the first seven days of intense grief and disorientation; friends may bring food for these days to help the family.

It is customary for a daily service, known as a shiva minyan, to be held usually in the late afternoon or early evening. This brief service allows the mourners to recite the *Kaddish*, the prayer recited in memory of the deceased. This can also be a time for publicly sharing memories of the deceased.

the act of tearing is an ancient ritual that serves several functions: 1) Since we are physical beings, we need to do something physical to express our grief; 2) It is a symbol of the tear in the fabric of the family after the death of a loved one; 3) It sets up a separation of status: prior to this moment, the mourners have had the responsibility of taking care of all of the details of the funeral and now their responsibility shifts to allowing the community to take care of them. As the ribbons/garments are being torn, the following is said by the mourners: *"Baruch atah Adonai, Dayan Ha-Emet - Blessed are You, Adonai, Truthful Judge."* Others may also recite the following passage from the book of Job: *"Adonai natan, Adonai lakach, yehi shem Adonai m'vorach - God has given, God has taken away, blessed be the name of God."* The ribbons or torn garments are traditionally worn on the outer garment for the first seven days of mourning- the period of shiva.

After a eulogy comes the *El Malei Rachamim* - This is a prayer that is usually chanted that mentions the deceased by their Hebrew name and states that they are "sheltered beneath the wings of God's presence." The congregation stands during the chanting of this prayer. In most cases, after the *El Malei Rachamim* is recited, the family exits the chapel and retires to the separate family room in preparation for the funeral procession to the cemetery.

Since the mitzvah of "accompanying the dead for burial" is so important, the act of placing earth into the grave takes on a very important role in the service.

After the service is concluded, the mourners return to the vehicle that will take them to the house where shiva will be observed. It is customary in some communities that the congregation forms two parallel lines facing each other, and,

Death in the Jewish Tradition

Jewish funerals can take place in a variety of locations. Some funerals are exclusively graveside; others occur in multiple locations-starting at the synagogue, or a funeral home, and then processing to the cemetery.

Traditionally, burial takes place as soon as possible-within 24 hours, although this is not always possible.

Jewish tradition teaches that the deceased should be buried in a simple casket. It should be completely biodegradable. A kosher casket is made entirely of wood - with no nails whatsoever. Embalming is also not permitted (unless required by law). The reason for this is so that the process of decomposition can take place in a natural fashion. Open caskets are not permitted at Jewish funerals.

Traditionally, mourners do not greet attendees until after burial. Prior to the service, family members and loved ones of the deceased will gather together in a separate room and wait until the service is about to begin.

Keriah (tearing)-Just before the beginning of the service, the officiant will gather the mourners together and place a black ribbon on their outer garment. (In some Orthodox communities, an actual garment is torn.) This is usually done when the family members are gathered prior to the service. In some communities, *keriah* is performed after the service and/or in public. The officiant may explain that

Or—to the usual solar intrusion
beneath the window shade,
to more taxes and arthritis
and sin.

By Mark Scheel

Published in *Star Chaser* (Anamcara Press, 2020). "I Sleep with the Dead" appeared in *The Kansas City Star*'s Poet's Corner.

I SLEEP WITH THE DEAD

Astrologers, priests and necromancers
long ago decreed
the living shall sleep north-to-south
aligned in harmony with the poles.

The dead, on the other hand,
are laid to rest
parallel with the sun's path,
but west-to-east, so as
(at the appointed hour) to rise facing
the Second Coming.

The dimensions of the lake cabin
where I bait my fishhooks
preclude those hallowed traditions.
I bunk down at night
west-to-east, positioned as if
stretched out in my coffin.

And always I wonder—
as somnolence takes hold—
will my eyes open next
to a supernal choir, to cherubim
and a lighted path to glory?

The earth is soft and damp. I scrape a small rectangular ditch with my hands. I pour the gray sand, the pallid gravel, the bone dust into it. I cover it up again, and re-lay the ribbons of ivy over it. I sit on a stone, and take out a sheet of lined notebook paper. Alone in Francis's woods, I read the names out loud: forty-two names of cats, dogs, and horses. Ours, my parents', my friends' beloved animal companions over decades of life. And I ask Francis to look after them, because we no longer can in this world. The glossy twist of black from my mare's tail is tucked into a knothole in the broken olive tree. The skein from my friend's gray gelding hangs from a root in a grotto behind a statue of Francis.

I cry, hard and for a long time.

In one of the chapels, there is a wooden box. There is a basket of paper and pencils, and an invitation to leave requests for prayers that the monks at Eremo will make to our friend Francis. I add a note to my list, I explain whose names these are, and thank them. I fold it up small, and tuck it into the prayer box.

Then I walk back down the hills into Assisi.

Footsore, heartsore, and filled with peace. By a story I don't even fully believe in, but I needed it anyway.

Pax et bonum.

By Julie Stielstra

neither purse nor scrip, nor shoes," and went barefoot. But when he was hobbling on bleeding, stigmatapierced feet, his friend Clare made him a pair of shoes. Clumsy, misshapen, leather desiccated and unstitched, they are unbearably poignant: a gift of love that even a zealot was kind enough to accept.

The next morning was brilliant and cool. I set off from a northeastern gate, the little square tin in my backpack. A quiet road switchbacked its way up the side of Mount Subasio. Groves of olive trees sloped down to the plain on my right hand. Birds sang. A car passed occasionally, but I was otherwise alone. It was uphill every step of the three miles to the Eremo dei Carceri: the hermitage of caves. When even little Assisi was too much for him, Francis walked up there. He lay on his back among the trees. He prayed. He meditated. He knelt in the grottoes and shallow caves worn into the hillside. As I panted my way along, I touched the corner of the tin in my backpack. I was doing this for a reason.

The place is pretty much exactly as Francis knew it. A few stone buildings perch in the woods. An ancient olive tree clings to the side of a ravine, bolstered and propped by roughlynailed boards: it has been there for eight hundred years, and they say it's the tree where the birds gathered to hear Francis talk to them. A cracked remnant of one of its thick limbs, knotholes partly patched with cement, leans against a parapet. I open the tin.

A dry rocky path leads up and away from the chapels. I walk in the green shade peppered with birdsong – birds I don't know the names of, as I would at home. A tumble of rocks forms a little corner ledge, trailing with ivy and fern. I might be able to find the spot again, if I returned.

I am not Catholic. I am not Christian. I am not a believer in any religion, never have been. I regard Christianity as one more set of stories and legends like those of ancient Greece, Rome, Persia, or native North and South American societies that fascinated me as a child. But who can resist the story of Saint Francis? Who preached to birds, who gentled a wolf through kindness and a fair bargain, who sang songs to the sun and moon, and felt that mud and flowers had souls? Who knew illness and imprisonment and suffering – and joy and ecstasy and love? I had come to pay my respects.

The great basilica has two levels. The upper is gloriously illustrated with frescoes by that pre-Renaissance genius, Giotto, who changed all of Western painting pretty much by himself. Handsome young brothers bustle about, the cuffs of their jeans and sneakers showing beneath the hem of their long brown robes. You step carefully down a narrow stair to the crypt. People are mostly silent. At one end of a small chamber – not much bigger than my living room and dining room combined – is a hollowed pillar, protected by metal grates. And there he is – buried deep centuries ago by his brothers, to protect him from graverobbers and souvenir hunters. The bones of that crazy, loving little man are there, right in front of you. People pass slowly around the pillar. They kneel, they pray, they cross themselves, they leave candles in the baskets to be lit by the monks. I sat in a squeaky wooden folding chair a few feet away and was the only one in streaming tears.

Upstairs is a collection of relics. Who can say for sure if they are genuine? There was a robe said to be worn by Francis: brown, rough, patched, and amazingly enormous. But if it is your only garment, it's helpful to have it be big enough that you can wrap it around yourself and serve as a blanket too. Francis took seriously Jesus's order to his disciples to "carry

ASSISI PILGRIMAGE

The ashes were in cardboard boxes, in plastic containers, and one pewter urn. Four cats and three dogs. Some had sat on the living room bookshelf, one on my bedside table. For years. They didn't actually give me much comfort. More a reminder – that eventually I overlooked most of the time – that they were all dead.

I spooned them into a pretty tea tin. Each being poured differently: like fine dry gravel, like whitish coffee grounds, or pale bone-sand that raised a wisp of dusty smoke from the tin. On top, I coiled two twists of hair, silver and glossy black, from the tails of two much-mourned horses who had given us 45 years between them. And sealed the tin. I hoped that a small square metal box in my suitcase would not alarm the airport x-rays or customs when I arrived in Milan, Italy. It didn't.

Milan to Florence on the high-speed train is about 90 minutes at 150 miles per hour. Then three and a half hours on a local, chugging through Arezzo, along the edge of the startling Lake Trasimeno, then disgorging students at Perugia before sliding quietly into the Santa Maria degli

Angeli station – a pretty little creamy yellow building with stuccoed walls and beamed ceilings. A shuttle bus groaned up a sinuous road to a tawny cluster of buildings at the top of an Apennine hill.

I was in Assisi.

We pour for our ***personal ancestors***. Those who gave birth to us, nurtured us and taught us. In particular, we pour for our female ancestors who have passed on – our mothers, grandmothers, great-grandmothers, those who carried us in their sacred wombs and infused us with their power. We pour…. Feel free to call their names…..(e.g. names of personal female ancestors) ***A'SE!***

We pour to welcome the present moment. We salute the power of the moment, and salute the ever present now….we pour… ***A'SE!***

We pour for our future generations. We remember them now and build for them, so that they can one day pour for us…we pour… ***A'SE!***

We pour to the seven directions to west, north, east, south, the up, the down and we pour for the ***CENTER – that which is Divine*** which dwells in each of us…we pour ***A'SE!***

We pour for the 5 elements: we pour for the f*ire, earth, air, water*, and the ***life*** that they all combine to make our material world… we pour….

A'SE!

We pour for each individual here as we ***as Sisters*** gather in this ***Sacred Circle*….. we pour ….

A'SE!

Which brings us back to where we started. We began with the Creator and we end with the Creator we pour 3 times …….

A'SE! A'SE! A'SE!

By Maaskelah Kimit Thomas

her family. Let's create and be that healing space for them, here…in our Village.

In the presence of our all powerful, all knowing, and all present Creator by whatever name you call It, we pour libations… A'SE!

We pour for our **Celestial ancestors** known in different cultures by different names. To some they are known as Orisha, to some they are known as Neteru, some of us call them Angels. We pour for them.

A'SE!

In the presence of our **ancient ancestors**. Those that existed *before* our **Maafa** – the fateful middle passage from the Motherland to this land. Those that existed before our captivity in this and other lands…those great and mighty ancestors whose names we continue to learn…..we pour…

A'SE!

In the presence of our ancestors who *died* during the middle passage and our Maafa, whose names we will likely NEVER know…we pour…..

A'SE!

We pour for our **Universal Ancestors**. The One's that researched and taught us who we are. Those freedom fighters that stood for what was and is right…. we pour… feel free to call their names….. (e.g. Harriet Tubman, Nat Turner, Mary McCloud Bethune, Malcolm X, MLK etc.) A'SE!

A Ritual: Libations for the Sisterhood

A Council of Elders is made up of senior leaders of local communities selected and designated by that community to act as a cultural and practical reservoir of community values, cultural and historical knowledge, as well as advice and support grounded in these. Included in its valuegrounding role, the Council is expected to provide rituals that support the community's development and healthful continuance. Women on the Council also bring an additional distinctiveness to this role.

Women have gathered throughout history, in nearly every indigenous culture on the planet. Perhaps it was for survival, for education, for nurturing and/or defense. The women have gathered. Have pulled themselves around each other like warm blankets and rays of strong love filtered through the magic and power that is **WOMAN**.

It is tradition that we gather, when one of us is in need of our collective healing energy and power - Energy and power we all have even when we sometimes forget – or perhaps no one has ever told us.

Yep. We are magic. And we are healers. One of the other. Each one to the other and collectively **WE** have the power to change things! **We** are those from whom human life flows. **WE** are the womb of creation. *Let us never forget how powerful we are!*

Even those of us who never physically bear children connect us to all the ancestors --- the women --- who came before us. **WE** are a powerful sisterhood. Let's wrap ourselves around this sister, Sister _____insert name____, and

Rituals and Religion

We segued into the worst kinds of death to work. We both agreed that suicides and the death of children were extremely hard. When these deaths were unexpected, families often went into shock. ("It can't be. There must be a mistake.") Tom admits to being exhausted both physically and mentally after a child's funeral service because he gives so much attention to detail; he wants everything just right for the parents.

Tom and I have different views on responding to the death of a person we have known. With him, the ongoing relationship encourages him to give extra-tender care. Knowing them is a benefit. For me, during my patrol days, it just increased my personal trauma. Big difference.

At Elliott Mortuary, seven days a week, someone will answer the phone to assist the caller in a compassionate and knowledgeable way. The phone call begins a process that leads Tom to between 400 and 500 funerals every year.

Tom is the first to tell you, in order for Elliott Mortuary to maintain its high level of professionalism, which includes earning peoples' trust, it requires each of its 25-30 employees (including seven who are funeral directors) to do their job, which is to do what's best for every family.

At age 61, Tom still has the desire to do the work, to help the families. Tom states: "The day we can't care for the families the way we have for so many years, is the day we should maybe not be in the funeral profession."

From my extended conversation with Tom Elliott, and after 40 years of doing business with Elliott Mortuary, it's no wonder that I firmly believe the business continues to be true to its slogan: "We do funerals but we build relationships."

By Jim Potter

Tom and I discussed whether people are exposed to more or less death today. We agreed that our society bombards us with images about death and dying on a daily basis. Whether it's breaking news reporting a homicide, fatality wreck, natural disaster, war, or the latest death count from a pandemic, multiple media platforms make the images and details nearly impossible to avoid.

However, an active shooter at a school who has learned to kill on video games may have no concept of real death.

The same is true today for a majority of beginning mortuary students. They lack hands-on experience working in funeral homes before making a career decision. This is due to a majority of the mortuary businesses having become corporate enterprises rather than the more-friendly, accessible, family-run endeavors.

Speaking of death, a considerable number of people would like to avoid planning the unavoidable. But those who take the time to pre-arrange their funeral service, help take the burden off of family members who may be emotionally spent. The idea is to plan your funeral while you're in good health, not when you're failing.

And for those people who plan on no funeral service whatsoever, Tom has a comment.

He believes that it's a disservice to family and friends to not allow them to celebrate your life. They may need the formal goodbye even though you don't think it's important.

Collecting human bodies is one of the duties of a mortuary. I mentioned to Tom that when I served as a deputy sheriff on patrol, I learned the scent of dead bodies. He agreed that there is no mistaking the odor of a decomposed body.

As mentioned earlier, "We have a true desire to do what we do every day, to help families in a meaningful and understanding way in a process that must be done. No family is void of this occurrence (death)."

Fortunately, shocked and grieving families don't need a mortician very often. Statistically, every 10-12 years a family has to make funeral arrangements. Given this lengthy period of time, it's understandable that family members need to be reminded of standard death procedures, from collecting the body to planning the funeral.

Tom Elliott was never pressured by his father, uncle, or grandfather to enter the familyowned mortuary business. However, when he made the decision during his junior year in college to join his father, he had a pretty clear picture of the work. Besides having spent a summer working at the mortuary, he had grown up becoming comfortable around dead people and about treating them and their families with respect.

Upon making his decision about his future, Tom started taking college science classes (anatomy, microbiology, pathology). The next year, 1981, he entered mortuary school.

There were 60 students in his class. Much to his surprise, only five were from families in the family home-funeral service. Tom recalls the instructor taking a quick survey. "How many of you have been to a funeral?" Only a few hands were raised. "How many of you have seen a dead body?" Even fewer hands surfaced. At this point, Tom was wondering about his fellow students. (Did they seem "abnormal" to Tom?) With so little first-hand experience, why were they attracted to mortuary school? He soon learned the decision was made out of curiosity, because it sounded interesting, and because they thought it would be cool.

I imagined Tom's childhood as being quite different than most, since his father was a mortician. But, as with most things, "normal" and "abnormal" are in the eye of the beholder.

Tom doesn't' recall his childhood being odd or different. He was taught to always ask if anyone was "in state," meaning a body was present, before walking through the mortuary—with or without friends ("who walked around with wide-open eyes"). Tom remembers how common it was to learn from his elders about the deceased person, including about his or her family—and on the business side—a thing or two about the type of casket that had been selected.

"What's her name?" Tom would ask. "How old was he?" "What did she die of?" All of those questions were answered by his elders.

"We wouldn't think anything of death calls," Tom recalls. "They were normal. It was never scary. It was who we were and what we did. Seven days a week, my father was on call," ready to respond to death. It might be Christmas dinner. "The phone would ring, my dad would answer." A minute later he'd say: "Honey, I've got to go."

Phone pagers and cell phones changed the life of morticians. Until then, after business hours, they needed to stay home to answer the telephone. They understood their responsibilities:

"A death has occurred. It's our job to respond and receive the body."

"It's our job to respond, to contact the family in an immediate and polite manner, to address questions or concerns for what needs to be done next."

"Well, I've talked to my kids," she replies. "On Friday, my grandson Billy has a soccer game, and one of my sons is going on vacation the following week. They said they had an opening on…"

And so it goes, Tom explained: "It used to be that in our society, when death occurred, we'd drop everything. It wasn't an inconvenience." But today a religious service is less important because fewer people attend church. Faith is less meaningful to them.

For these reasons, cremation has grown in popularity. Like a memorial service, a cremation allows the family to schedule a gathering for a later time, especially if the death occurs during a pandemic.

When Tom joined his family funeral home business in 1981, locally only 2% of human bodies were cremated. By 2019 the rate was 50% and it will continue to increase, believes Tom, as family preferences continue to adjust to a changing world, including less expensive choices.

In the big cities, cemetery property is expensive. Outside of Hutchinson, in Reno County, one cemetery charges only $5 for a grave space, but another cemetery, closer to town, charges $1,600. At the latter location, digging a grave is $1,500. And the cost of a monument ranges from $500 to $5,000. You can see how a family can spend $6,000 at the cemetery before even discussing the actual service.

When one compares cremation to a traditional burial and service, the difference in flexibility and price is considerable. Some people will bury their loved ones in a traditional graveside ceremony, while others choose a special location to scatter the remains. For those who are indecisive, they can keep the ashes until the decision.

any plans for a formal goodbye were drastically altered. Suddenly, carrying out the wishes of the deceased was often impossible. Instead, family members were forced to compromise, making decisions based on state guidelines, not personal plans.

"Let's just cremate her, we'll have the service later," said one customer after discussing the limited choices during a pandemic.

Another family member asked, "Why spend $10,000 on a funeral if only a few people can attend?" (To be clear, that price includes cemetery costs for a plot, digging the grave, and adding a monument.)

Elliott Mortuary owner, Tom Elliott, doesn't mince words: "Funerals are expensive." And he understands the appeal of younger families looking for a bargain, seeking out the lowest price for an immediate cremation.

Tom understands the business. He knows that many people don't care that his family has been serving the public as morticians for generations. But he's also clear about the future: "I'm not going to be a discount funeral home." He and his staff have a "true desire to do what they do every day to help families in a meaningful way in a process that must be done." They won't lower their professional standards.

Times have definitely changed since Elliott Mortuary was established in 1935. "Death for some families today is an inconvenience rather than sacred," he states. In those cases, a family often wants the funeral service to be done as simply as possible.

"What date you have in mind, Mrs. Smith?" asked the funeral director of the widow.

Interview with a Mortician: The Best Morticians Serve the Living and the Dead

Tom Elliott, 61, is a fourth generation mortician who has worked 16,000 funeral services in the last forty years—without getting jaded. Today, he continues to show the empathy and compassion expected and desired by family members and friends of those recently departed.

I sat down to talk with Tom—with his quick smile—in the lobby of the chapel at Elliott Mortuary, Hutchinson, Kansas. He was his typically personable self: cheerful, courteous, friendly, helpful, and engaging.

Another thing about Tom, I've never heard him called by his last name. Not, "Mr. Elliott." Not, "Elliott." Just, "Tom." You see, he's seemingly on a first name basis with *everyone*!

I soon learned from Tom how COVID-19 had upended the funeral service industry across the country. I'm not talking about something as simple as wearing a mask or gloves, or social distancing. During the pandemic, families who wanted to bury a loved one, to carry out his or her last wishes, were stymied with limitations that didn't exist before the spread of the virus. The other effect was a big financial hit to the mortuary business.

In thinking about one's funeral, most people would expect at least ten people to attend the event, but the pandemic changed that reality. For a period of time, families had fewer choices in selecting a funeral service. Once the state began mandating no gatherings of ten or more people, ways we disappoint even those closest to us. It's part of who we are. My prayer for each of you here today is that you will seek reconciliation. Someone said, 'The truth will set you free, but first it will make you miserable.' Talk about the truths of your relationships. Talk with each other honestly. Wade through the misery truth-talking stirs up. And let your love for one another thrive, honest love. It is not easy. It takes courage. But that love will deepen when you cultivate truthfulness in your relationships."

I had no idea where I found those words. They just came.

After a pause I invited people in the congregation to come forward and share brief stories of Don as they knew and interacted with him. I don't recall what people said, only that many came forward. Some of the stories were funny and we laughed, others were sobering. People spoke emotionally of how he had helped them, of his generosity with his time and his money.

When the room was again silent, we sang another hymn, had a prayer, and the service ended. I came down the chancel steps and directed the family to exit first. Mrs. Anderson approached me and took my hand. "Thank you," she said. "I don't know how you were able to do that, to guide us to a full remembering of my husband, but I am very grateful."

"I don't know either," I told her. I didn't say that my own long-deceased father got me through that funeral, or that my chance encounter with <u>DON</u>'s son and the truth he told his father's mourners rearranged my understanding of the death trade.

By Gretchen Cassel Eick

"My father—<u>DON</u> Anderson--was a good man to many of you. He liked people and could be generous at times. But he was also a bully to his children, especially to me. He refused to let us be ourselves. And, Mama, if you are honest, you know this is true. You never criticized him, but he bullied you, sometimes abusing you verbally, and I won't let him go without naming this." He took a deep breath and the microphone picked up a ragged exhale. "To be completely honest, his death brings me relief. I don't have to keep apologizing to him for being different from him. I don't have to pretend we are a happy family. I don't even have to stay in this city any longer. You can keep your tributes and your admiration for this man, but for me, I am better off with him dead." The man had become tearful and wiped his eyes with the back of his hand at this point, then walked rapidly down the chancel steps and out the nearest door.

I heard a noise, breathy and extended. It seemed the mourners were letting out a collective sigh, as though they'd all been holding their breath ever since he started up the chancel steps. No one even whispered. All eyes were on me.

I stepped back into the pulpit. My legs stopped shaking. I looked out at the stunned faces before me. I didn't know what I would say. The words just came.

"Funerals are difficult. Each of us has an autobiography we would like others to know that is part facts, part denial, and never the whole truth of our lives. Because we each have dark places, things we wish we had not said or done. As we have heard from Don's son, this was true of Don Anderson. We come together today to remember his life, and his son has reminded us that it is important to be aware of the whole picture, how Don—and each of us—has affected others. The

After a hymn, a scripture reading, and prayer, I approached the pulpit on legs that wanted to walk me out of the sanctuary. I took a deep breath, then I launched into a summary of Tom's life. Trustee of the church, president of the local YMCA, leader of the annual fund drive for United Way, CEO of Fidelity Bank--the accolades poured out of me and I began to relax. I could do this.

I sensed more than heard people stirring in the pews. The deceased's wife was weeping. The deceased's children sitting on either side of their mother were comforting her while the eldest son, sitting at the end of the pew so he could easily get out to make remarks for the family, was standing. I had only begun the eulogy. Was this a common practice? He started to approach the pulpit, but his sister held him back, gripping the sleeve of his suit. She stage-whispered he should sit down. He shook her off and pushed me out of the way.

I think I stopped mid-sentence. Theological school never taught us how to do funerals or what to expect. They never told me the family might cut me off mid-eulogy.

His face was ruddy and his eyes bloodshot. His voice was husky with emotion. *"My father's name is <u>Don</u>. You can't bury a man and get his name wrong, Don, DON, D-O-N."* Now the daughter stood. Was she coming to the pulpit, too?

"Please forgive me," I stammered. "I have been deaf all my life and rely on lip reading and hearing aids." I pulled out the hearing aid in my right ear and held it up as evidence. "I messed up. Perhaps you'd like to make your remarks now?" It seemed obvious that the man had no intention of standing down. He glowered at his mother and his angry eyes scanned the assembled congregation. Then he spoke.

Being a divorced clergyman selling liberal Christianity to a church in a conservative suburb of Cleveland, Ohio in 1950 was as uncommon as walking on the moon. But he found Mom and his underachieving sperm, with her energetic ovum, made me. It was a good life. Until the morning of April 9, 1971 when I was fourteen.

Dad and Mom had awakened early. Dad was talking about the day ahead of him, about to get up, when his heart cramped and stopped beating. Mom pounded on his chest and gave him mouth-to-mouth, but she couldn't revive him. I remember opening my bedroom door to see him being wheeled out on a gurney, Mom in her robe stumbling after him. At 57, he just stopped. It was my first encounter with death. Like Dad's presence at the rally in Nuremberg, it redirected my life.

It left me confused and angry. How could I know this larger than life man, who entered a room and drew every eye to his charismatic 6'5" self? He had preached hundreds of provocative sermons, performed hundreds of bedside vigils, met with families going through sacred transitions, performed memorable funerals for loved ones, and become a community icon. Over time I decided I could access my father by walking in his footsteps.

A decade after his death I graduated from the seminary he had attended and became a minister in the same American Baptist denomination. Within a week I conducted my first funeral and entered the death trade.

I didn't know the man I was committing to the dirt, but I was determined to write a memorial homily.

The church was packed. The man was obviously beloved and important.

Had they walked another way, Dad would have pursued a career in insurance. He would have stayed with his wife. They would become an ordinary middle-class American couple who tolerated each other and perpetuated his father's attitudes toward materialism (*It's good*), Jesus (*The only route to Heaven*) and divorce (*It's unacceptable*). By accident they heard the dangerous man, saw the power of hate, and broke the mold of his father's stolid, small-business Republicanism. They became progressive activists, F.D.R. Democrats, and passed that identity to their descendants.

I benefitted from their chance encounter with Evil. Without the flood of questioning it opened in Dad, his tired guppy-sperm would have stayed put and died.

They returned to the U.S. on the last American ship to leave Italy, traveling in total blackout to avoid German submarines. During that dark passage Dad got sick and almost died. Along with progressive politics, he had acquired rheumatic fever in Europe. It left his heart permanently scarred.

When you know your life may be brief, it's easier to make otherwise impossible choices. Dad left the insurance business for a career in the church. He made no money but treasured the close personal contact with people at their most holy moments and time for researching and writing each week as he prepared sermons. It stimulated his intellect and creativity. He also left his wife, who had anticipated a more affluent life.

talk with a wagging finger and screaming his version of the truth with total self-assurance. His audience loved it and him. The crowds, who had survived the Great War and the dismantling of the German Empire, fed like hyenas on his combustible words.

In his letters home Dad described the rally, half-a-million people devouring Hitler's hate speech and yelling for more, gorging on his dramatic declarations that Germany would be great again. They loved the Great Betrayal narrative that Germany was done in at the Paris Peace Conference in 1919 by the Others of the world—Jews and Asians and Africans. Hitler told them that brown and tan people from across the world had sat at a table in Paris and dismembered their Homeland. Germans could not even attend the conference determining their fate. Their emperor, their navy, their industrial might, and their colonies were stripped from them, and they were fined $33 billion in reparations they must pay to the nations that defeated them in the Great War.

The course of individuals and of nations is continually changed by coincidences like the one that took my father and his wife to that Nuremberg rally. They chose that morning to follow masses of people along the wide Grosse Strasse to the Reich Party Congress Grounds. There they discovered an enormous crowd gathered to hear the Fuhrer address a Nazi rally. *They happened upon the rally quite by accident.* It is the way of life: What may appear to be a minor coincidence alters everything.

A professor says you'll never make it in this career, and you drop out. A national leader takes offense at another national leader's tone, and diplomacy is replaced by war. My father and his wife happened on that rally, and the political views of generations of my family changed.

The Death Trade

It wasn't the vocation I had planned. No. You might say it smacked me upside my head at fourteen and hasn't let me go.

I was my father's caboose, the third and final product of his sperm. I picture a small cluster of guppy-sperm struggling like last-gasp swimmers to reach Mom's womb, calling out to each other in fragile, end-of-life voices, *"It's just a little bit farther. We can do this."* Fortunately, one fell into the ovum he was looking for, breathing heavily, and staggered to the soft wall of my mother's uterus, where they remained locked in an embrace for the next nine months. Luckily for me they made it. Dad might not have had it in him for another try.

Heart problems had haunted him thanks to rheumatic fever when he was fresh from the Continent. They had traveled through Europe in 1939, he and his first wife, wide-eyed twentysomethings seeing the Motherlands prior to studying in Switzerland with the best and the brightest young theologians from around the world. *Except, it was 1939.* That nasty, selfabsorbed, mustard-gas-damaged man with the scrub brush mustache had become The Next Great Thing.

In Nuremberg they had watched him bellowing promises to restore Germany to greatness and rid it of the people who had brought it down—the communists and queers, socialists and foreigners. They saw him punctuating his incendiary

Once, when providing a final pastoral visit as a hospice chaplain to a Spanish woman of faith, I was welcomed into the home by the gathered family and immediately ushered to the bedside to provide requested spiritual comfort. Surrounded by her very loving family, also people of faith, the patient sat on the side of her bed, buffered by pillows since her physical strength was quickly waning. The room was full, hushed and reverent. I had entered the cathedral of mortality. I expected sobriety and prayerful silence, and I prayed the words of my mouth and the meditation of my heart would be acceptable to God, the family and the patient.

I got what I prayed for...and more.

Kneeling before this woman, I took a deep breath and looked into her eyes and began to feel my own eyes watering, and I calmly said, "Ahh, Senora."

Seeing my deep feeling for her and my respect for the circumstances, Senora took my hands and, catching her breath as much as her beleaguered lungs would allow, looked at me and said,

"Ahh, John. All four of my tires have gone flat!"

It took only a nano-second to grasp the gift she gave all of us in that room as we broke into amazed laughter. She was using metaphor as she stood at Death's door! Life and Death danced in that one statement, and it was the very opposite of depressing, morbid or unbearable sorrow! While not all deaths are so poetic, I am forever changed by this one act of great kindness.

By John Monroe-Cassel

Bedside Cathedral

In my decades of spiritual leadership through primarily pastoral roles in hospice and church ministry, Death has knocked at many a door and stopped for so very many people I had come to love and cherish. One would think, as many have shared with me, that such sustained presence at people's dying and death would lead to depression and unbearable grief.

It has not. Quite the opposite, actually.

The landscape of loss has many travelers upon it, and when there are this many people who have given and received love, there are many stories about life, and often these stories evoke less interest in dying and death than about living! We all know at some level of knowledge and intuition that we will die. This is not breaking news. For many of us who bear witness to life in extremis, the often courageous way people go into Death's embrace is deeply, deeply moving. Sometimes, the way deeper into the landscape of loss includes a bit of humor, as well.

Ghom, the Sanskrit word (pronounced 'whom') is the root word for human, humility, hummus and humor. It is a word that provides us with the earthiest nouns available in the English language! I have borne witness to several deaths in which humor was the foundational expression of the dying person as well as tear-laced cheer of the surviving loved ones, honoring the death with the humor given them in such precious last moments.

lives. Police officers who consider self-harm like suicide -- the #1 cause of police officer death -- could be thrown a psychological lifeline. And decreasing the number of emotionally ill officers who would contemplate using a level of force inappropriate and/or illegal when interacting with all people in their community, would mean the public could be spared many unnecessary life and death encounters at the hands of the police.

As strange as it may sound, when mental health measures aren't taken to assist police officers after they encounter death, death keeps on killing.

By Jim Potter

A portion of this essay is from Potter's police memoir, *Cop in the Classroom: Lessons I've Learned, Tales I've Told* (Sandhenge Publications, 2007).

to push me forward and encourage me, if I hesitated.

My law enforcement training did not prepare me for dealing with death, especially the psychological burden of watching a person die while I was trying to help save a life. My investigation and emotional overload didn't stop at the end of my shift at 7 a.m. when I went home and changed out of my uniform.

I knew I wasn't alone, but that didn't help me. The circle of people affected by death extended beyond the fatality victim's family and friends. Witnesses, EMTs, fire personnel, and police officers, were also, to some degree, traumatized, if not victimized.

Sleepless nights, anxious moments, poor concentration, a short-temper, and a fixation on the fatality wreck, were some of my ongoing symptoms. I personally diagnosed myself with a mild case of Post-Traumatic Stress Disorder (PTSD), but I never sought help. I reasoned, *it's not that bad; it's just one of the negative consequences of being a deputy sheriff. I'll live with it.*

Unfortunately, people with PTSD often remain in the environment that causes the stress. So, continuing to work fatality accidents, suicides, or lethal force encounters in a toxic environment is a disastrous formula.

There have been many improvements in caring for the walking wounded since my retirement from law enforcement. I imagine there's still a negative connotation for officers who seek help, but help is available, and it's required more often by agencies after specific types of confrontations.

If police officers received better psychological care, I'll bet they would overwhelmingly respond more appropriately in high-stress encounters. Having healthier police officers would lead to better policing. Better policing would save

The driver was confined in the metal cage of wreckage. Movement of his head and shoulders was the extent of his freedom. He swayed slowly, rhythmically, back and forth, as though he instinctively knew he was caught in a trap and needed to escape for his survival. Even though his body was moving, he was never conscious. He didn't talk, but gurgled.

I said a few words to the severely injured man, quietly telling him that we were there to help and to hang on. As I looked for a way to assist, checking the extent of his bleeding, my prayers were not answered. Examining his head with the beam of my flashlight, I saw his right ear framed in its bright rays just before blood began flowing from the inside, swirling, filling its cavity. Before my eyes, he was dying from internal bleeding. *Could he be saved?* I wondered.

He died at the scene, still trapped in the vehicle's wreckage.

Working that motor vehicle accident was a great emotional and psychological burden for me. At the deadly scene, I gave more time to the victims than I did the suspect. I was no EMT, but I had wanted more than anything to help him live, even if my contribution was only holding a spotlight for the ambulance and fire department teams. When he died, part of me died. Thankfully, I didn't attend the autopsy.

There was no preparation in my law enforcement training for watching someone "expire," but in looking back, there was an early clue. It was when my chain-smoking sergeant on our fatality-wreck run had recognized the enormity of an officer's first official encounter with death.

At the scene, he had ordered me to look at the body. He had been preparing me for what would be worse, yet to come. Like a mother fox with her young, he was conditioning me to a harsh environment and allowing me to practice my survival skills while he was nearby, looking over my shoulder, ready

As I stared at the corpse, still a person to me, all I could think of doing was to say a prayer for her. But I made sure not to close my eyes or bow my head. I wasn't being evaluated for my spiritual side. The department had a roster of volunteer chaplains available upon request and I wasn't looking to fill their shoes. I wanted to learn the ropes of a patrol officer. This meant complying with the sergeant's order.

Upon completing the interviews and investigation, I was surprised the death hadn't bothered me as much as I had expected. Since our county had been having a rash of fatalities, other officers had told me that the worse ones were those with small children and people you knew. *Maybe that explained why this death wasn't affecting me much, I thought.* Or, maybe *I'd have a delayed reaction.* I'd always thought of myself as a sensitive person. Now I was wondering if this was callousness or some natural, protective shield to personally and professionally guard me from the stressors of anxious encounters.

The answer was a year in the future. I hadn't seen someone die, yet.

No fatality accident or wreck affected me as emotionally as the one I worked just a year out of the police academy. The difference between viewing a corpse and watching someone die was indescribable. The feeling of helplessness and hopelessness was all consuming.

I was the first officer to arrive at a two-vehicle head-on crash where I found one driver in critical condition, pinned in his vehicle, bleeding from his nose, mouth, and eyes, with labored breathing. The driver's wife was injured, lying on the ground beside the car. She asked me if her husband was going to be all right. I tried not to show my fear as I told her, "We're helping him now."

New to the profession, I had a lot to learn, especially about death. One of the requirements of the job—both then and now—is learning to be comfortable enough with death so that an officer can maintain focus on the work. Unfocused, the investigation is incomplete and unprofessional.

Growing up, I was fortunate to have a healthy family around me. My closest experiences dealing with death were when my pets died, and when I attended funeral services of distant family relatives.

Although my father was a World War II veteran, and had a "war trunk" with European souvenirs, I never asked him the main question on my mind, "Did you ever kill anyone?" Thinking back, a better question might have been, "As a medic, how did you learn to cope with death?"

During my early patrol officer training, I specifically remember one early morning when I had a chain-smoking supervisor as a passenger in my patrol car. We received notice from emergency dispatch of a "10-40," or fatality car wreck, on the far side of the county. Driving through thick fog, it was my job to get us to the scene as quickly and safely as possible. The sooner we arrived, the sooner we'd be able to protect the accident scene, help with the injured, and try to prevent another accident from occurring in the hazardous road conditions.

There were other officers assisting us at the scene, but one of my duties was interviewing the driver who had apparently driven left of center, causing the fatality accident. Prior to that, my sergeant ordered me to have a look at the body of the deceased, who had been ejected from her vehicle.

The sergeant was observing me, watching for my reaction.

Living Death

When I was hired by the Reno County Sheriff's Office (KS) in 1981, there were some patrol officers who were suspicious of me. For starters, I didn't drink, smoke, or eat meat. But worst of all, I had a college Master's Degree. Some of the officers even called me "Doctor Potter," instead of "Deputy Potter," thinking that I had earned the academic title.

At the time, and it's still true today, the minimum educational requirement for many law enforcement agencies (at least in rural America) is a GED or high school diploma.

After I was hired and in uniform, sooner or later, a patrol officer would mention in my presence that no matter how smart someone was, no matter how many college degrees he or she had, a person couldn't be successful as a deputy sheriff or police officer unless they had common sense. I never disagreed.

A standard question in law enforcement job interviews has always been: "Could you shoot someone, take a person's life, if the circumstances required it?" Basically, departments don't want to hire anyone who can't pull the trigger if their life or another person's life is in danger. (Considering the state of law enforcement today, another valuable question would be, "What would you do if you observed an officer using unlawful force against an unarmed citizen?")

Some things are impossible to predict. Another area of concern to the road sergeants, our supervisors, was how well a rookie officer would deal with death. I didn't realize it at the time, but this was certainly a valid concern because it can easily become a mental health issue.

Death Professionals

TO REMEMBER

In December of 1991, noted author, Isabel Allende received disturbing news: her twenty seven year old daughter, Paula had been rushed to the hospital. Paula and her family had known for several years that she had inherited a rare metabolic disease: porphyria. Now the disease had caused her to lapse into a coma.

Paula remained in a coma for many months, and Mrs. Allende was there at her side until she died. Paula never regained consciousness.

In order to help her heal her pain, Isabel wrote about her experience. At one point Mrs. Allende wrote: My grandfather once told me: *"Death does not exist; people only die when we forget them."* Then Mrs. Allende continued: *"It is wonderful what memory does. You can remember how someone smelled, you can remember the tone of their voice, and re-create the person to carry inside of you."*

Paula, too, appreciated this essential function of memory. Knowing that her rare disease might claim her life prematurely, Paula wrote a sealed letter to her family. Mrs. Allende could not bear to open that letter for many months, but when she did, she found comforting words that recognized the power of memory. Paula had written:

"I know that you will remember me, and as long as you do,

I WILL BE WITH YOU."

By Richard Eick

Death as jazz. That is the piece my brother and I played at the end of his life. He was the percussion and I played the melody. It was all improvisation and call and response played as duet. And our family and friends, a small tight group, jammed with us as we played the last movements.

We dished and argued but we didn't talk much. Neither of us had the skill of knowing what we needed, much less the ability to express it. We grew up wishing people could read our minds and would give us what we needed without having to ask. Perfect practice for death by improvisation. We worked in code and by signals. For a time, close to the end, it was a cacophony, but at the end, when it mattered, we both were at our best.

I learned to feel while losing my brother. I had to let the emotions happen. There were so many that I would have broken and would never have been able to finish his life with him. He never had the chance to let his feelings go. He was too busy keeping the beat going, staying alive. I have often felt as if I am experiencing the feelings of two, as if he left me with the resources he never had time to use. Each day since, his life and his death have been the background refrain as I composed the rest of my life, without him, but with all that he left with me.

By Susan Moir

Suite for the Bull and the Fairy

My brother Hank died of AIDS thirty years ago. He was 41. I was 43. He was 2 years younger than me until then. Now I am 72, but he will always be 41.

Hank was his gay name. It didn't suit him that well. It sounds strapping, so athletic. His family name was Henry, and it's much more like him, small, charming, and yet, somewhat aloof. But I called him Hank because that is what he wanted to be called and I believe that people should be called by any name they want.

We were not close when we were young. We were both equally surprised at my coming out as a lesbian and him as a gay man. We came out in our late twenties and together, he shortly after me. Our family was chaotic and very close-knit, but we were always apart from the rest. We became very close in the years we were apart from the rest and together in our gayness. I have been apart by myself for a long time now.

A year after Hank, Dizzy Gillespie and Rudolph Nureyev died on the same day. Although Nureyev, like Hank, was too young to die—a gay white man who died of AIDS even if they were not saying so at the time---and Dizzy was an old Black man, it was Dizzy's death that day that brought me back to my brother. The jazzman, familiar by his first name, not the classicist who kept secrets to the end.

As amazing as it was that Mr. Cheatham had saved that paper was the paper's impact on all of us who knew Nancy. It was as if we'd found a tangible piece of the person who'd left us 12 years ago. It was an example of how nice it can be to find memories of lost loved ones still shining in the hearts and minds of people around us. And how seemingly meaningless items can ignite powerful memories.

By Mark E. McCormick

Published in his book, *Some Were Paupers, Some Were Kings: Dispatches from Kansas,* 2nd edition (Blue Cedar Press, 2020).

Hours later at Barry's parents' house, Barry, his sister Donna and their mother, Shirley, poured over the sheet, touched by the gesture and amazed that someone would have saved the paper for all these years. It listed, in Nancy's small, neat handwriting, her name, her parents' names and jobs, and her siblings, oldest to youngest.

Donna guessed that the man who'd delivered it must have been Val Cheatham. He taught gifted students at OK Elementary School, which the Sanders kids and I had attended. Curious, I looked him up.

Mr. Cheatham (that's what I've always called him) explained that he'd long kept scrapbooks of his students. It began, he said, when he once split his pants doing calisthenics with some students. At the end of the year, one of the students sent him a patch with a clever little note attached and his memory library was born.

The books make for great reference material when former students write to reminisce. "I can look back and tell them little things about their hobbies and who they were in class with," he said, smiling through the phone. "They think I have a great memory."

He remembered Nancy, and when he learned Barry would be in town, he retrieved the book of Nancy's mementos. He found the sheet he gave to Barry among group photos and scenes from plays she'd performed in.

Mr. Cheatham, now retired, said he asked students to fill out the sheets because he was interested in how family size and birth order impacted personality. Nancy, he said, was soft-spoken and aware of things beyond her age and knowledge, and she wrote stories rich with personal detail.

She was a bright, thoughtful child.

[Barry] Sanders Blindsided—Gift from Teacher Ignited Powerful Memories

Waiting in the back of a long line at North High School last weekend, many people worried if Barry Sanders, scheduled to autograph books from 2:30 to 4:30 p.m., would pull his early retirement act again. But he hung in, scribbling in the last book sometime after 9.

Barry had shown up in a giving mood that day but would receive a gift he never saw coming. The event— complete with honor guard, spirit squads and one heck of a marching band— had been planned around the life of one special person, Barry's older sister Nancy.

Nancy Sanders, to whom he dedicated his best-selling book, *Barry Sanders: Now You See Him . . .* , died in 1991 at the age of 27 from the autoimmune disease scleroderma. Proceeds from the day's book sales and donations benefited scleroderma research. Barry surpassed his goal of raising $10,000 (he has raised $14,500 as of Wednesday) and gave hundreds of people warm memories on a cold day.

But there was someone else there also in a giving mood. After about four hours, a man in line unceremoniously presented Barry with a worn sheet of paper. The man said the paper was a worksheet of Nancy's he'd saved from her time as his student in the early 1970s. Barry, who's as composed as Kansas City Chiefs' Coach Dick Vermeil is weepy, looked up, clearly moved. No sooner than Barry had said thank you, the man had dissolved into the waiting crowd.

I watched Krissy's body melt into relief and relaxation with the receiving of this message. She really heard the words and believed them.

I want to make it clear that I am not a trained medium. I am just a woman who listens to what is being shared beyond this immediate reality. We all have this capability. We can all be one another's angel messengers.

Our loved ones who have passed speak to us in limitless ways. Through symbols like coins and feathers, with messages spoken by other people, and of course, through music like in this moment. These are signs of affirmation that we are always connected and closer to those who have passed than we might sometimes believe.

We must be willing to listen to the music that is flowing through us and around us. And as Krissy's mom reminds us all when we live this way and remember what is true, then through our deepest and most pervasive grief, we can still "Walk on, walk on with hope in your heart. And you'll never work alone. You'll NEVER walk alone."

By Cora Poage

"Walk on through the wind," I continued to sing. "Walk on the through the rain. Though your dreams be tossed and blown."

Krissy started to mouth the words with me, her hand on her heart.

"Walk on walk on with hope in your heart and you'll never walk alone. You'll never walk alone."

We were both crying now. My body was tingling, my heart so open. We looked at each other with such awe and recognition, as she attempted to speak.

"Cora, that song." She said. "How did you know?"

"Know what?" I asked. "It just kept playing over and over in my head so I sang it."

"That is the song that my mom sang to me EVERY night before bed," she shared. "And even when I went to college, she would call me and leave a recording of it on my dorm room answering machine. That was OUR song."

Shivers overtook my entire body. And I knew.

"Krissy, your mom is here. And she is so proud of you and wants you to know that she always taking care of you and with you." The words just flew out of my mouth before I had a chance to second guess them.

I breathed into the space between her tears, her longing, her Remembrance. I sent her nurturing, care, and love through my energy. As I inhaled and exhaled, the same song from before came back with persistence.

I doubted and questioned my next step.

"Do I say something?" I wondered. "Will that just impede her healing process? I don't want to make this about me. What do I do?"

So I followed my gut, heart, and soul. And spoke up.

"Krissy, may I sing a song that just keeps playing in my head? I know this sounds odd and I've rarely done anything like this in a Coaching Session, but I feel to share it."

She nodded, "Of course."

It was a song from my days of performing musicals in my Kansas high school. A song I hadn't thought of for over 20 years. "You'll Never Walk Alone" from the musical "Carousel." I began to sing, "When you walk through a storm hold your head up high. And don't be afraid of the dark. At the end of the storm is a golden sky and the sweet silver song of a lark…"

Krissy began to sob, her body shaking with emotional release.

Grief and Music

I felt a bit crazy. As an Intuitive Coach, I am familiar with the mystical and magical. I am accustomed to receiving messages from Angels, guides, and other realms. Yet, this moment was something new and even unnerving.

As the Coaching session unfolded, I could hear faint music playing in the background of our conversation. We were speaking over Facetime and I even checked my iphone to see if my music was accidentally playing through the phone.

I held back from mentioning the song that was reverberating over and over again in my mind and heart. However, as I listened to my beautiful client share about her treasured mother who had passed on years ago, the musical notes permeated my Being.

It was the Anniversary of her mother's passing, and my client was sharing that she was so surprised that all this time had passed, and yet she was still experiencing the grieving process.

"I just miss her so much," she expressed, the emotion catching her off guard, her words cracking to pieces. "Sometimes I feel like I am still a young girl that just wants her mom."

Silence is overflowing,
And heartache is a wellspring.

Time oozes on forever,
The perpetual tyrant of
This broken-Promised Land,
Wherein there dwells
No milk. No honey. No words.

by Cammie Funston

No Words

When the human heart
Plummets from elation to devastation
In the blink of an eye,
There are no words.

When hope rebounds
From heaven's ceiling to the cellar of hell
In a blinding flash,
There are no words.

When dignity has bowed
To spread palms
In the path of aborted jubilation,
There are no words.

When the flames of courage
Are suffocated
In a coarse blanket of reality,
There are no words.

Grief is a wealthy sovereign.
Agony and anger,
Flow from her breasts.
Her coffers are piled high with despair,
And her gardens burgeon with fear.

In this place, so rich with sadness,
Solitude is plentiful,
Tears are abundant,

and sit across the table from all the empty rooms of his life,
have a conversation with what or whoever might have
filled them, if only he had done this instead of that, called

heads instead of tails, if only the universe had been
a square dealer. Stooping, as my dad always did
when the glint caught his eye. "Lucky penny,"
he would say, grinning like a kid at Christmas,
and in those two words were more of the

Great Depression than in any history book ever written.
Even now   the Devil whispers it in my ear as I reach
for the plastic cups: "Lucky penny," and since there is no
bridge here under which to pull over until the sobbing stops,
I go back into the aisle of the frozen and retrieve my father's voice.
It sings from my pocket on the drive home. It serenades me still,

from its place on the shelf next to the John Tesh CD I picked up
the day after the night of the bridge, an aria daring me

to write it.
To feel
lucky.

And when I glance up from my computer
and out the window at a thousand silver pennies,
the rich night wrapping this round planet
like the warm blanket of my father's arms,

I do.

By Robert L. Dean, Jr.

(First published in *Flint Hills* Review)

Clean up on Aisle Five

A glint of copper from the floor separating
Hungry Man from Marie Callender. My father
trying to communicate with me again. I say

"again" like it happens all the time and not just when I'm
least expecting it, the last time being some twenty-three years
ago, 2 AM, driving home in a tux from a gig and the night
all dressed in mourning, crying, even, raining the tears
I have yet to shed in the six months since he died, and

there he is, aural ectoplasm extruding from my car radio,
manifesting himself in the saccharine alto sax voice
of a John Tesh tune I hate. Devil's advocate is what

he called it, and he played the part whenever he could.
Vietnam, Watergate, Reaganomics, the earth is flat,
you only think you love Jenny, Pamela, Susan. But
that is not why I pulled over under a bridge that night until
my sobbing and the song and the rain and the whole damn séance

ended. Not why I pass up the penny and move on
to the aisle of plastic utensils and paper plates
for the lonely eater. No, I am concerned with
appearances, moth-eaten as they may be in my case.

What would people think? A sixty-something man,
stooping to pick up one cent as if it might make
the difference in the rent this month, or the car payment,
as if it were treasure enough to take himself out to a restaurant

Since his death, I've noticed how so many people have a photo with the Champ or a story about meeting him. It has kind of lost its cachet. But I will of course cherish my story because its symmetry seemed to so perfectly align with the arc of his life. The shadowboxing and playful overbite. Drawing people to him. Baking a cake for a child he'd accidentally frightened. Throwing a private birthday party. Performing a magic show.

And then, in the quiet of his mother's dining room, he takes the time to share the wonders of his faith with a stranger and then cares enough to send him off with a most cherished gift.

Ali gave the world so much. It's no wonder so many of us—the once-frightened boy, me and a billion others—feel such a tremendous loss in his passing.

By Mark E. McCormick

Published in his book, *Some Were Paupers, Some Were Kings: Dispatches from Kansas*, 2nd edition (Blue Cedar Press, 2020).

As the boys and the teacher later filed out of the house buzzing, he extended his hand and as I shook it, he brushed my cheek with his and said "Asalam Alaikum." When I returned the greeting, "Walaikum Salam," he seemed stunned. "Are you a Muslim, brother?" "No, but I know about the greeting," I said. "Wait here," he said, and disappeared down a hallway. He returned with a Koran and a Bible. He sat me down and for about an hour, pointed out numerical discrepancies between Bible passages. A first reference to an assembled army might say 5,000 soldiers while a subsequent reference would say 50,000.

Then he asked why Christians tampered with the Bible so much. A King James Version. A New King James Version. A Good News Bible. A New International Version. This is the foundation of your faith, he said, and you alter it several times a year? "The Koran is the same today as it was when Muhammad brought it down from the mountain," he said. This had never occurred to me. It felt profound. He seemed so sincere.

I eventually lifted my journalistic mask and told him he had long been my hero and that I would appreciate this meeting for the rest of my life. I added that while everything he'd taught me felt compelling, I wouldn't be converting to Islam.

He smiled. I told him I needed to go because I was the only reporter working that day. I wanted desperately to beg for an autograph, but couldn't bring myself to do it. As I stood up though, he reached into a long box of his boxing trading cards. He signed two of them, folded his handwritten list of Bible verses he'd scribbled for me to study around them, and handed the entire trove to me.

Ali: Speaking to a Loss Shared by Many

2016

Muhammad Ali often made surprise elementary school visits in Louisville, Kentucky, his hometown and where I began my journalism career. One such visit at his niece's school prompted a hasty assembly.

"Who's the baddest kid in the school?" the Champ rasped, biting his bottom lip, settling into a boxing stance and stirring the air with his fists. In unison, the children pointed to a boy seated next to his teacher. Ali waved him down from the bleachers to the floor for some playful shadowboxing.

But one of the first things you immediately notice about Ali is his size. When he snatched the heavyweight title from Sonny Liston in 1964, Liston had to look up at the 22-year-old challenger in the center of the ring before the fight and got acquainted with the young man's hamsized fists.

If Ali loomed large physically and figuratively to adults, he looked like a mountain to that child. With a slight Ali feint, the frightened boy bounded back up the bleachers and into his teacher's lap. Ali, we were told at the newspaper, felt terrible and later asked the teacher about the boy. She told Ali that the boy was fine and was about a day away from his birthday. Ali reflexively invited the boy and a couple of friends to his mother's home for a private party.

As the Saturday reporter, I got the scoop. The Champ baked the boy a cake. He magically pulled quarters and ribbons from his ears and in a grand finale, stood in front of us and appeared to levitate.

I'll be back when it lets me breathe again.

Enjoy this photo.

See his happiness?

I'm not giving in, I'm stepping back.

    Wear your mask. Wash your hands. Keep your distance. Do your research. Be a responsible person.

Find hope. And foster it.

I'll be back.

By Jeani Rice-Cranford

I still hear his voice in my head when life goes full tilt. I still want to tell him about the really great things when they happen. And I would love to hear his laugh in person again and not on some video recording.

But I can't help that I also feel glad he doesn't have to worry about Covid19. And I can't help but feel glad he doesn't have to see daily updates of atrocious human behavior.

He would have worried about all of us.

Since he can't be here, I'm glad he's still with me in some way. I feel him--but of course it's not the same.

This is my Papa. Harley Ray. He was in the Army. He drove soldiers to the front lines in WWII.

He was a truck driver and worked on farms. He loved dogs and nearly every one was named Stormy. He loved popcorn and chocolate--yes, together. And westerns. I'm sure he'd seen them all. He had 8-tracks when I was a kid and I'd listen to them while he mowed. He smoked a pipe. He wore aftershave and bolo ties. And boots. He loved his boots. He had big belt buckles. And he wore his baseball cap tilted to the side--the way I sometimes do--because it felt better. And he loved us. Fiercely. Completely. Unapologetically.

I know he didn't always understand my actions and my decisions. But he always believed I'd get it together.

I miss him.

I'm tired of feeling defeated and despair. I'm tired of reading about foolish decisions and bullying and overt racism from the occupant in the people's house. I'm tired. And grief is here. And it will linger for a few more days.

Grief

is strange, isn't it?

It never lets you forget it's always with you.

Nine years ago, we took this family photo. There was a knowing, I believe, in all of us at that time. Something we just sensed.

Before the weekend was over, before my mom and sister (and her children) could travel back to Kansas--while I returned to Tennessee--we'd spend several hours late at night in a hospital waiting room. We watched terrible cable TV. The kids tried to sleep in waiting room chairs. And we tried to occupy our fearful minds with humor and memories.

We would learn that night he was preparing to leave this realm. Several days later we'd all find ourselves back in Illinois by his side.

If you would have told me on this day nine years ago that I would figure out how to keep pushing forward into all life had to offer without my anchor physically present I would have called you a liar.

He would have agreed with you though.

He would have told you what he always told me.

That I'm smart. And I'd figure it out.

I miss him every day. I think of him every day. I'm so glad my momma is here with us in Tennessee. It helps make him feel closer.

"The secret is in the bulbs," she tells me. "You can water it … or not … and it will keep on growing."

"Eternity plant," I repeat dumbly. She nods.

Eternity. And now Dad is there … here … there. And I water him every week—just a little bit, when my computer's task reminder chimes at me. ("Every time you hear a bell ring …")

And I say a little prayer for him. With him. To him.

Even the nun says that is okay.

By Julie Ann Baker Brin

Where he first learned the art of growing living things, a craft he perfected after 45 years of working on the farm, then the greenhouse, then the plant nursery. He could grow anything—anything—keep anything alive. And how he would talk about it: the daylilies he tended, the geraniums transplanted, the acres and acres of whatever feed crop was good for the soil that year ... and on and on, to the point where my Mom and brother and I weren't necessarily listening but happy in his excitement of triumph over the elements. To see the glow in his eyes as he pointed out some small, rare, wild beauty. To share in his modest, peaceful joy. And that must have been all he needed from us.

You'd think with that near-constant exposure to spontaneous botanical lessons one of us would have retained a nugget of wisdom or three, would at least have a green pinkie if not thumb. Alas. The rest of us have a comical, if not shameful, knack of killing nearly every potted plant we acquire within the season. At first I thought that should probably make me feel guilty, make me repent and change, start learning everything I could about plants and their plant-ly ways. As a tribute to Dad. Who will carry on the knowledge? So much knowledge. Where to start? A botany course? An herb window kit? A tomato plant? Who am I kidding?! The last six plants I received (mini roses, violets, calla lilies and more calla lilies) committed assisted planticide before I could even hang them to dry for potpourri.

No, the eternity plant is the only thing I've kept alive. The plant I got after demanding of the first greenhouse clerk I could find: "Give me a plan I *cannot* kill." Wiping her hands on her smock she led me confidently to the small, unlikely-looking plant (to me, looking like any other ordinary green thing).

ENDLESSNESS

Today I told the nun about my Dad growing in my office. I figured, even if she didn't believe me, at least she wouldn't laugh. (That was part of her job, right? She *couldn't* laugh.) "I believe you," Sr. Sophia said. And I believed that she believed me.

But I can't quite believe the fact. Shortly after Dad died I came to work to find him growing in my office. My eternity plant (common name for *Zamioculcas Zamiifolia*), after being the only being I had managed to keep alive for eight years, and never having done so before, had sprouted a shiny new branch. It was bright as spring disavowing the winter. Its thick, waxy leaves greeted me: unmistakably, undeniably.

"Dad?!" I whispered, dropping from my hand whatever I was holding, whatever dutiful chore I was attending to. Of course it was him. The terracotta pot was surrounded by mementos of my grieving: the well-intentioned cards, the candles, the angel figurines gifted to me. As if I really needed physical objects as reminders. But this one physical object—this growing, living, verdant, fertile, tiny abundance of life—would be the quintessential reminder. It is, truly, a part of Dad, just as surely as if I had put his ashes in that planter.

But there were no ashes to be had. His earthly body is in a poplar box inside a steel vault down in the old Baptist cemetery by the reservoir of his childhood. Where his first farm used to be, before it was intentionally flooded.

Grief and Remembrance

Death happens.

Death is the final
destination.

It creates a parallel
world which resembles
the one left behind.

By Bill Dee Johnston

AS I GROW OLDER

I want fifteen (for now) important items
tended to in a timely manner:

Trim my toe nails
Trim my finger nails
Trim nose and ear hairs
Make sure my socks are clean
And my underwear, especially my underwear
And my glasses
I want my hair cut handsomely short and neat
    like my scotch
I want my children, grandchildren and
    great grandchildren to know I
    am alive until I am not
Find the damn democrats some GUTS
Somewhere
Ask Cora to explain "SELF AS SOULMATE"
Treat every faith and non-faith
    Community carefully, we are
    all terribly wounded
I am a "veteran of the cross" so see
    if some money can come of it
When I stop laughing
    Someone pick up where I left off
Do you have any questions?

By Michael Poage

MOTHER'S FEARS

Reading to my dying mother, I chose
A poem by Donne, the cry of triumphant
Christianity. The last lines close
With the end of death, with life abundant.
But there is a catch, the Tinkerbell Clause.
Donne's triumph only comes if you believe.
Does weak acquiescence to God's ten laws,
And weekly church attendance equal belief?
It is too late to ask – the tubes remove
Her ability to talk. Tied down by IV's,
She cannot even gesture. The reproof
In her grey gaze is now an urgent plea.
She is afraid, but of what? Of dying?
Or of not being allowed to die?

by Janet Jenkins-Stotts

A Good Life

Don't stare at me
with pity and concern
at my bent over back
at my slow shuffling steps.

Yes, I'm slow and curved
and dull and tired.
But I like who I was
and I was who I liked.

I lived my life
wearing red and purple;
riding horses, climbing hills.
I danced the tango.

I worked and played.
I lost, I cried.
I loved and laughed and
I lived. When I die

on my tombstone inscribe:

"I was here
Now I'm gone
I had a good time." *

By Judy Keller Hatteberg

*Quote from Barbara Kingsolver interview with the *Daily Beast*, July 2017.

You take us in your arms. Rock us. Suckle us. Sing to us. Lullabies of time and space. In your eyes, we see ourselves, tiny, naked, reaching. There now, you say. There.

When the doctors come down from surgery they flash thumbs up. She will sleep a while, they say. Go. Sup. Break bread.

In the restaurant, phones ring. Come back. Malfunction. Failure. Oh, come back, quick. The waitress floats towards us with the check. We bundle on our funny suits, slip into hyperspace. Hearts implode. From our eyes, stars fall.

By Robert L. Dean, Jr.

(First published in *Flint Hills Review*)

you. Redeem you, as if you are an object of desire on a cereal box and all we need is enough box tops. We are told these devices will anchor you in our world, on our planet, for another five years. Ten, if lucky. Without them, you will, again, at any moment and without warning, without any chance of return, fail.

We say yes. Yes, to everything. Yes, and as soon as possible. Yes, and yes and yes. We are selfish. We are weak. We are afraid. We love her, we say. We can't live without her. Repair her. Please. On our knees, we say it.

For a week, for an eternity, we watch with you in shifts, our eyes peeled for signs of departing spaceships. The only way we know when they go is when you no longer mention them. Act as if they had never existed. As if they have wiped all trace of themselves from your brain. We act as if, too. We are happy to see them go. Or would have been, had we. Maybe even waved, bye-bye.

Thank you for not taking our mother, our wife, to see your leader. Go in peace.

You review the schematics. You are impressed. You are hopeful. Your mind is sharp. Clearer than in years. You embrace the devices. Sign your life away. The doctors high-five. Or would, we suspect, if we weren't here. We suspect. Have begun to suspect. We count our box tops and come up short. The doctors pull box tops from their pockets. They look foreign. Cryptic. Alien. We suspect. We plot. In the middle of the night we will smuggle you out. Hide you in the basement. The garage. For as long as you last. As short as. We are selfish. We are weak. We are afraid. We love you, we say. We can't live without you. The forms. Rip them up. Burn them. On our knees, we ask it.

Spacemen

In 1992, Eileen Dean departed this life, not once, but twice. This is a telling of the days between.

When you see them outside your window we breathe a sigh of relief. You ask what they are doing out there on the roof in those funny suits, floating around like that. The first words you have spoken since your malfunction. Construction, we say. Maintenance. Though we don't really know. We can't see them. We haven't, like you, been to the other side. If you've ever seen spacemen before, you haven't mentioned them. If we could track these particular spacemen down, look out through your eyes, drift in the ether of your slowly returning mind, we'd shake whatever passes for their hands. Ask them in for lunch, figuring hospital food is the same no matter the planet. We question the doctors about the spacemen. They say it's normal for someone coming back from the dead.

The doctors huddle with us. Speak in whispers. Sketch out variants of your future for when the spacemen return to their home planet, as we are assured they will. The doctors wear long white coats and have appendages dangling from their necks. You ask if they too are spacemen, snuck into your room through the air conditioner vent. We too wonder, sometimes.

The doctors want to implant things in your body. Experimental, otherworldly things. Top secret. Forms will have to be signed. Consent given. We are shown diagrams. Schematics. Artist's renderings. We are told these will save a self-taught expert on American Indian cultures with years spent traveling to reservations to oversee bilingual education programs. She says she is proud of you.

You are not sure what her words mean but they sound caring. There is something about being sorry for all the years she kept you out of her life. You understand when she says that she loves you and is grateful that you are her mother. Good, now you know who she is. She is your daughter, the one in the framed photo you carried with you as you traveled and placed on the bookcase in each apartment. Only that photo is of a child holding a teddy bear and this woman has not been a child for a very long time. You are glad that she is here holding your hand.

The two of you are alone in the room and both quiet in the dim light. Curiosity is wearing you out. You are tired but you don't want to leave her. It wouldn't be polite. Women of refinement don't leave their guests alone. *"I will be OK,"* she tells you. *"We will all be OK. You don't have to stay any longer."* Her expression is earnest and concerned. *"Are you ready?"* she asks, not expecting an answer.

Your breathing is erratic, but your eyes take it all in, the woman, the room, the bits of memories that surface and sink. She stands, stroking your hair. For some reason neither of you understand, she moves her fingers on your forehead, making the sign of a cross. *"God bless you,"* she says. *"I need to use the bathroom. I'll be right back,"* she says. Then she rushes across the hall.

Your eyes slumpse down. They are glad to give up their sentry duty. Your sigh is shallow and protracted. When she returns minutes later, you have left. It was fitting and proper and it was time.

By Gretchen Cassel Eick

A man enters the room, tall and gentle, wearing jeans and a sports jacket, white dress shirt and tie. He, too, seems kind. You see the woman beside your bed smile as though the heavy burden that rounds her shoulders and pulls down the corners of her mouth is lifted just by seeing him. He passes her something to eat and says he will take the monks, whatever that means. He holds your hand and says calm words. It takes so much effort to understand what is being said to you. You try to squeeze his hand just a little. You are glad he is there. After a while he leaves.

Now the woman beside your bed fiddles with a box on the table and the room is filled with Puccini's *La Boheme*. Ahhhhhhhh! You know this! The music lifts you off the bed. You are floating, relaxed and full of joy. You can no longer feel your toes or your fingers. The center of your body feels warm, like sitting before a fire.

That other woman comes into your room, the one from Hosp...? Hospital? Hospice? You have seen her before, you think. She sometimes comes and speaks to your daughter (if that is who that woman is). Gently she pulls back the covers to uncover your legs and feet. She shows the other woman that they are cold and mottled. Then she covers you up. She says something about the heart holding on, all the warmth focused there as bit by bit we let go of life. Is that what you are doing? You have stayed awake a very long time, not wanting to miss anything. They remark on this. *"Do you think she is afraid?"* the woman asks. You want to tell her you are NOT afraid, just curious, like you have been all your life.

Dusk arrives, then night settles in for the duration. You and the woman sit in silence and she strokes your hand. She is talking to you, telling you what an amazing life you have led—one of the first head start teachers, a novelist, an artist,

The women who take turns caring for you in this house are very kind. They have not known any women who have written books or whose landscape paintings are good enough to hang on the walls throughout the house. The chubby red haired one— is she a nurse?--is especially kind to you. She comes in now, her smile gentle and her eyes damp. You used to tell her how nice she looked and thank her for her care for you, but lately you cannot locate the words. She turns you onto your side saying something about not wanting you to get something-- you cannot make out her words. She smells of chocolate. Ah, how you love chocolate! She talks to you and that woman while she refreshes your bed, plumps the pillows, changes the bag that holds yellow liquid. Then she leaves.

Yesterday (Is that right?) the woman beside you brought two Buddhist monks in orange robes to chant for you. You recall them sitting beside the bed, that woman behind and between them. They were chanting something you did not recognize. It was not your "Naam Yo Ho Ren G..."? You cannot remember what it is that you chanted during all those decades when you chanted every day. That woman brought the monks because you are Buddhist, but Japanese Buddhists don't wear saffron robes.

The monks' visit brought the other residents to your doorway. Nothing like this had happened in their Midwestern lives. The caregivers, too, came to peek in, taking time away from the quiet celebration of Angie's 93rd birthday in the living room.

People look at you with curiosity and with respect. You enjoy the celebrity although you don't understand it. The larger monk shows you a small audiotape. He is leaving it for you, *"to help you leave this material world."* You don't understand the meaning of his words, but you do understand his kindness.

few making it through the mesh and few of them any longer recognizable.

A young woman with two small children enters your room, takes your hand, and speaks gently to you. *"Hello, Grandma Virginia. You remember Ivan and Kara? We wanted to see you again, to tell you we love you."* The children eye you curiously. They are dear with their dark hair and eyes, beautiful faces, tentative smiles. This is probably a new experience for them, seeing an old person unable to talk propped up in a bed, eyes blazingly wide open. You know that you have seen the three of them before. They are charming and you attempt to smile, always your default when around children. You have no idea if the muscles around your mouth obey you, if the children can tell that you are smiling. They stay briefly, then depart. The children's kisses brush your hand like butterflies landing and taking off effortlessly.

"Mom?" From the doorway the young woman glances at the older woman seated beside you. *"I need to get the kids some supper. Will you be all right here by yourself?"* she asks.

You are confused. Who is Mom? Your Mother? This woman beside you? The young woman? And what is "by yourself"? Your questions dissolve in the darkening air of the small bedroom.

Are there things you must do? You vaguely remember that you have manuscripts to complete, but they seem unimportant now, here. Money? No, you haven't paid a bill in several years. Someone else does that for you, perhaps she who is still nameless— Mom?--who is sitting beside your bed.

Everyone treats you so well, you young Americans who have money to spend while Europe is still struggling with economic depression. You are both 26 and ecstatic to be having this adventure. If war comes, it will only increase the excitement of your year abroad, you are sure of it. You attempt to bring back memories of that time, but you recall only murky images from photographs you took—snapshots of your friends at the Institute who came from all over the world and left suddenly, summoned home by worried families.

You remember a blurred picture of a crowd listening to Hitler in Berlin. You snapped it just as they raised their arms in the Seig Heil salute to their Fuhrer. You recall a photo of Sam and you standing on either side of another American--you think he was Tracey Strong, head of the YMCA. Why can you find his name when you don't know the name of the woman sitting beside you?

You recall your hastily snapped photo of the Italian ship you found passage on at the last minute in November, the third month of the Second World War. You remember the green Swiss countryside dotted with light brown cows and trees covered with fat red apples. And children with apple cheeks and lederhosen, racing across the meadow. You remember the damp and salty darkness of the blacked-out ship on which you returned across the Atlantic, and the fear that cramped your stomach that the missiles in the ever-present German submarines that prowled the waters would find you.

An amorphous anxiety creeps over you. There is so much you want to recall. Not clear why you cannot. Half-memories, disconnected and slippery, move into and out of your mind as though your thoughts have been stirred together and poured through a small-holed sieve, only a

loved you. Not a complicated love. Easy. Finally, after two unsuccessful marriages and several verging-on-serious boyfriends, an easy, reciprocal, undemanding, unjudging love! That woman (Is she your daughter?) tells you that he has called every week to talk with you since she moved you away from him to this house near her. Same message each time. Not much to report. Connection is what matters. You smile inside hearing his voice. Does your smile show? Can he hear it? He says good-by and that he will see you.

You are drifting again. Daddy rarely comes home. When he does, he goes straight to the room he shares with your brother, sleeping on a cot in Jack's room. Jack fills his afterschool hours with sports. That's how he escapes your mother's simmering anger that sucks all the oxygen from your home and makes life there intolerable for all of you. Your escape is aided by a fellow student from your high school, Sam Cassel, the eldest son of the owner of the Feed and Seed Store, one business not affected by the Depression. Farmers always need feed and seed.

Sam was tall, handsome, intelligent, and a good conversationalist, like you. Someone who would be Somebody. He could take care of you the way your daddy had taken care of you in his prosperous years. So you married him. Now you and Sam are on a ship crossing the Atlantic Ocean, embarking on the most exciting year of your life.

You stand at the prow of the Swedish oceanliner soaking up the Nov of it. The sea air thrills you. You are en route to Sweden. From there you will make a leisurely tour of northern Europe, eventually arriving in Geneva, Switzerland at the Ecumenical Institute where you and Sam will be students for the next year. It is 1939 and Europe is electric with rumors of r.

money short of street walking— my friend pays me to run her boarding house at the shore in the summers and I take in laundry. Now we must pull you out of Goucher College. I swear, Virginia, I could have coped with all of it, but this...? This I cannot forgive. I cannot love a man who betrays me. I deserve better than this!"

You have never heard your mother talk for this long. She is a private woman, withholding and introverted. Then she does something you have never seen her do: she cries. You are confused, dizzy with this new and devastating information about your father who you love more than anyone. You cling to your anger at your mother. You hate her for belittling him, chiding him, treating him with disrespect, casting withering glances at him whenever he enters the room. You find excuses for this letter.

Perhaps he never reciprocated. Perhaps this other woman was not a woman at all but only a love-sick teen with a crush on your father. Perhaps he only kept the letter because he needed it to remind him that someone believed in him and wouldn't criticize him.

Far away you hear a telephone ringing. The woman who has been sitting next to your bed, the one you think is your daughter, speaks with a person on the other end of the line. She holds the phone to your better ear and says, *"It's Reuben. He wants to talk to you."* Reuben. Familiar name. Familiar voice, deep and a bit raspy. *"Virginia, this is Reuben. I miss you. When are you coming back? Your daughter says you don't talk any more, but I know you can hear me. I think you are spectacular. I love being with you. I love your laughter. I love it when I put my hand on your thigh and you tell me you are not that kind of girl."*

Reuben! You remember! The tall Shoshone man who lived in the same retirement complex, the man with whom you ate meals and watched tv. You loved Reuben and he not his fault that he is gone so much, working as a traveling salesman, driving long days and nights from town to town peddling baking equipment for his company.

Your mother turns on you, her handsome face distorted by anger, the beautiful mouth set ugly, lips pulled in so they are only a narrow, tight line. Her eyes spark hot fury. Her voice is low and intense and demands your careful attention. *"Your precious father is a liar and a cheat. The man you idolize is despicable, a shadow of what you think him. I know."*

Your hands seek your ears, cover them, and push hard to keep her words from entering you. You refuse to listen. But her words pry through your fingers and her enraged face is etched on your retina through your tightly closed eyes. *"LOOK at this!"* She forces your hands from your ears and pries open your fingers. She shoves a letter into your hands and, when you refuse to read it, she tells you that it is a love letter to your father from another woman. She found it in his pocket as she was preparing to launder his trousers.

"Do you know that I made my own living before I married him? Made beautiful hats for the rich and famous. Then I helped him impress his boss so that we moved up into their ranks. Living high, we were, your dad a vice president of the biggest baking company in Philadelphia. You and Jackie could have anything you wanted at Wanamakers. I made sure you took classes in music and painting. Jackie had his own pony. Life was good until the Crash. Then he suddenly had no job, until he convinced the baking company to allow him to sell its products door to door. He was pitiful. He stopped smiling, stopped his Irish banter, stopped the flirtatious way he used to have with me. He only smiled when he talked with you and Jackie. I was the one who arranged to sell the house and located this small apartment, though I am embarrassed to be seen in this neighborhood. I do whatever I can to get

that time. Only that the doctor, your psychiatrist, told you that staying in the marriage would mean returning again and again to the hospital.

That was helpful. Who would blame you for walking away under those circumstances? Only, they did blame you, almost all of them. No matter. You did what you needed to do to survive.

Who is the middle-aged woman sitting beside the bed? She looks familiar— dark hair and eyes strikingly intense, a perpetual frown giving away her uncertainty about what to do for the fragile, bedridden woman you have become. Could she be your only daughter? Your caregiver tells you she has brought you here to be near her and her family. She looks like she carries the weight of the world on her broad shoulders.

Before your fall she took you to a bookstore to see a display featuring her new book. She has told you that she is in charge of two big conferences over these couple of months. She's worried about all that she must see to in addition to her teaching and being with you. Her frown is not unpleasant or critical, just burdened. You feel for her taking on so much, including you.

Sometimes you cannot remember why she is here or who she is.

Could she be your mother? Her regal bearing and coloration are similar, as is her figure, statuesque, but rounder. Probably not. Your mother's frown conveyed disapproval, especially of you.

Clouds cover the sun, darkening your room. Your mind carries you to another time and place. You are eighteen. You have found the courage to stand up to your mother, to tell her that it is not right the way she treats your father. It is

Departing

For Virginia Cunningham Cassel, 1913-2002

You lie in the hospital bed in a pleasant enough bedroom in a ranch house in an unfamiliar city. You are half your normal size. You fell sometime in the recent past and broke your hip, but at 88 the doctor advised not submitting you to surgery. Clearly something else is gradually sucking you out of your body, so why put you through the pain of hip replacement? Anyone can see you are being eaten away.

Vaguely you remember a Nature documentary about how frogs can be paralyzed by a certain water insect who proceeds to eat the frog from beneath the water while it is still alive. Bit by bit the insect devours the frog from its inside and the frog is incapable of resisting. Finally, only its skin floats on the surface of the pond. Is that what is happening to you?

The days run together as you sit propped up in your hospital bed enjoying the sunshine that pools in your lap and envelops the room even in these gray, indeterminate days of winter. The quality of the Light. When you were painting you paid close attention to Light, analyzing and experimenting to recreate it just so. Now you simply absorb its warmth and enjoy.

Some days lying here you recollect another hospital bed in another city where they bound your arms and legs and applied electric shocks to you. Your doctor thought it might cure you of your chronic unhappiness in your marriage, might bring you back to that vibrant young woman Sam had married ten years before. You have no clear memories of

Hank's Last Night

I wish that I had stayed but there
had been many nights and I did not
know this was the one.

I missed the signs.
When he said his friends who had gone before are
here and they are speaking to him.
When I said good night and he said I love you.

He had ignored me, not spoken to me in weeks.
Spectral thin, he wandered from room to room
in conversations from a haven of his special making. I
was a ghost he walked through and around.
Angry because I had *done what I had to do*
--at the time--
to pay the rent and do the paperwork.
My act an insult and betrayal of his freedom and
his belief that there would be no end.
That he would go on.

The call at 3 am
The darkest drive and he was no longer here Just
hours after he told me he loved me.

By Susan Moir

to. She was torn. She couldn't imagine what it must be like to lose a child. Would talking about Wes help? What if talking wasn't something that his family wanted to do? "But that's what he wanted me to do," she said. She couldn't save Wes. Couldn't comfort him much, either. But if she could somehow honor his dying wish, maybe that's comfort enough.

By Mark E. McCormick

Published in his book, *Some Were Paupers, Some Were Kings: Dispatches from Kansas*, 2nd edition (Blue Cedar Press, 2020).